HULL DAILY MAIL

A Part of the Community

by
Barbara Robinson

with an added chapter
by
John Markham

Highgate of Beverley
Highgate Publications (Beverley) Limited
2009

British Library Cataloguing in Publication Data.
A catalogue record for this book is available from the British Library.

ISBN 978-1-902645-53-7

Highgate of Beverley

Highgate Publications (Beverley) Limited
24 Wylies Road, Beverley, HU17 7AP. Telephone (01482) 866826

Produced by Highgate Print Limited
24 Wylies Road, Beverley, HU17 7AP. Telephone (01482) 866826

Introduction

This book was intended for publication as part of the celebrations of the Centenary of the *Hull Daily Mail* in 1985. It took me four years to research and compile it, but it was completed in good time and handed in, together with a collection of photographs and other graphic material. When the time came, however, it was decided not to publish it, and a different programme of events was substituted. Fortunately, the script was not destroyed, and in 2006 it was found in the back of a cupboard at the newspaper's office and returned to me with permission to publish it myself if I wished to do so.

So here it is!

The title, 'A Part of the Community', was chosen to suggest a kind of sequel or follow-on to another *Hull Daily Mail* publication, the immensely popular *A North-East Coast Town*, telling the story of the Hull Blitz. The theme which developed as I worked was to show how the newspaper had somehow wrapped itself round the lives of the people whose stories it was telling day by day – for there were few citizens whose activities, from a simple birth announcement to a heroic sea-rescue or a sordid murder trial, did not at some stage feature in its pages.

Yes, the script was unashamedly promotional: that was its purpose, to sing the praises of the newspaper and advertise its century of public service. But not at the expense of truth. Every historical detail was as accurate and factual as it was possible to make it. The cut-and-thrust of board-room politics, the machinations of ruthless Press barons were all faithfully recorded.

It might be argued that the story would be made more readable if some of the detailed descriptions of production methods were left out, but for the historian these could well be the most important parts. The book shows how, in 1985, a large provincial daily newspaper was actually using a whole gamut of print technology reaching back to the days of Gutenberg and the medieval lithographers, through the innovations created in the Industrial Revolution and on to the introduction of the newest photoset methods.

Each working day, the starting-time was 9 am, and by 1 pm the first edition was on the streets. No wonder we called it 'The Four Hour Miracle'!

HULL DAILY MAIL
A PART OF THE COMMUNITY

A HUNDRED YEARS IN THE LIFE OF A PROVINCIAL NEWSPAPER

TO HULL AND GRIMSBY NEWSPAPERS, who have provided me with a fascinating career for no fewer than 37 of these 100 years, and to colleagues who have assisted in its preparation, this history is gratefully and affectionately dedicated.

Acknowledgements

The Men that Carry the News, Guy Schofield (Cranford Press, 1975)
Mark My Words, Mark Goulden (W. H. Allen, 1948).

Mr R. A. Brewer, MBE, *History of Hull Newspapers*,
Mr Ernest ('Tim') Underwood, MBE,
Mr Vic Moorhouse,
Mr Arthur Clarkson,
Mr Harold Wright,
Mr Jack Rooms,
Mr Brian Taylor – *Sport – A Growth Industry*,

And numerous colleagues, past and present, who have contributed to this work.

All illustrations by courtesy of Mail News and Media.

Contents

A Century of Service

It might be said with some justification that a city gets the local newspaper it deserves. For good or ill, whether it be tied to a political party line or not, a newspaper must inevitably, by its nature mirror the scene around it.

For 100 years, through staunch Conservative beginnings, through ownership which owed its origins to the Liberalism of Lloyd George, and on to the complete independence of party political allegiance which it enjoys today, the *Hull Daily Mail* has, through its consistently impartial news services, held such a mirror up to the city from which it takes its name, and to the surrounding area, whether it be known in the hearts of the people as the East Riding of Yorkshire and North Lincolnshire, or on the Statute Book as the County of Humberside.

'Love Hull, love the *Hull Daily Mail*' seems to be the pattern of life here. The newspaper's critics, in the main, appear to be those whose roots are not in the local soil, and who do not fully comprehend the customs of its people; those who adhere to extreme political views, whether of Left or Right; and those who are so absorbed in a personal cause or interest that they cannot understand why it must find its own, perhaps very small, place among the myriad other causes and interests which the mirror must find space to reflect.

But, love it or loathe it, most people domiciled in its circulation area read it, and are not slow to let the Editor know their views!

The history of the *Hull Daily Mail* is the history of Hull and its environs over the past century. Its circulation area, covering ground on both sides of the estuary, could have been best described as 'Humberside' long before the controversial reorganisation of boundaries in 1974 brought that county into being. Perhaps that is why, while giving copious space to the East Riding lobby, the newspaper by and large, followed a policy of 'giving Humberside a chance'. It also resisted movements to bring the cumbersome and confusing title, 'Kingston upon Hull' into general usage, and doggedly stuck to good, plain, four-letter 'Hull', the name by which the City is known all over the world.

'All over the world' might, indeed, fairly describe the *Hull Daily Mail's* true circulation area, for, whether posted to exiles on subscription, sent out by loving relatives back home, forwarded in diplomatic bags or through consular, trade or commercial agencies, the paper reaches pretty well every corner of the earth, penetrating far beyond the Iron and Bamboo Curtains as well as throughout the EEC countries, the Americas and the Commonwealth.

Development and Disaster

Hull has escaped the worst of the economic depressions of the past 100 years, but has also failed to share in the best of the booms. It was saved from mediocrity, however, by the development of a 15-mile system of docks which enabled it for many years to enjoy the distinction of ranking as Britain's Third Port, and by the evolution of a fishing industry which, in its heyday, boasted the world's largest bulk fish landings.

The years also saw the establishment, in the 1920's, of a University College of character and merit, which received its charter in 1954 and has since grown into a University which, despite its apparent lack of social impact on the community, is well-respected in educational circles, has been a centre for much quiet but useful scientific research and has offered a number of unusual courses ranging from Drama to South East Asian Studies.

City centre developments such as the moving of the massive William Wilberforce monument, and the creation of Queen's Gardens out of a disused dock, or the transformation into the sweeping vista of Ferensway of a warren of mean streets which had once seen a rooftop chase between the local constabulary and arch-criminal Charles Peace are all duly recorded in the pages of the *Hull Daily Mail,* now on microfilm in the newspaper's library and duplicated in the city's Local Studies Library as well. For local newspapers are an invaluable source of material for the historian; they record the happenings of the time and their impact on the lives of ordinary people with much greater detail and poignancy than even the most sophisticated of today's alternative media, radio and television.

Never is that poignancy more potent than in times of disaster, and if Hull has escaped the extremes of economic depression, it certainly has not dodged the horrors of war or the ravages of repeated losses on land and sea and in the air.

In 1904, 10 years before the outbreak of the First World War, the people had a grim foretaste of things to come when the Russian Fleet, in what could have been a farce worthy of the pen of a Peter Ustinov had it not had such tragic results, fired on a fleet of Hull trawlers in the North Sea, mistaking them for warships of the Japanese, with whom the Russians were then at war. It might have developed into an international incident, but King Edward VII was not known as the Peacemaker for nothing; he had a word with his Imperial cousin, compensation was negotiated, and oil was duly poured on the stormy waters around the Dogger Bank.

The King was popular in East Yorkshire, where he had been a frequent visitor as Prince of Wales, first as the guest of Christopher Sykes at Brantinghamthorpe and latterly – and disastrously – of the shipping magnate, Arthur Wilson, at whose fine, and then recently completed home, Tranby Croft, the infamous Baccarat Scandal, which was to rock the British throne, had its origins.

While the idea of the heir to the throne gambling for high stakes in the home of a commercial Johnny-come-lately might have upset Queen Victoria and the British people as a whole, there was a good deal of sympathy locally, both for the bon-viveur prince whose private relaxation had been so unnecessarily dragged into a scandal, and for Arthur and Mary Wilson, especially since the true reason for the sudden break-up of that Tranby Croft house-party had been Mary's bereavement through the sudden death of her brother.

The Wilsons had brought wealth and employment to the district – and, through their involvement with the County set and High Society, a touch of 'class'. So elegantly did the Wilson ladies wear their gowns that their dressmaker, Madame Clapham, of Kingston Square, shared in the limelight, and for a while Hull became an international centre of fashion, even Queen Maud of Norway having some of her dresses made in the Clapham work-rooms.

Other industrialists left their mark upon the City in more philanthropic and tangible forms – T. R. Ferens, James Reckitt, Joseph Rank and many more – and their deeds were duly recorded in the local press.

The 1914-18 War brought terror to Hull and other Yorkshire coastal areas in the sleek, deadly shape of Zeppelins, and these airship raids were so well documented in the *Hull Daily Mail* that it was possible to recall them in a fascinating series of articles more than 60 years later.

In 1921, Hull was the scene of a unique and spectacular disaster when the R38 airship broke up over the Humber, and the city's newspapers vied with each other to be the first with a story which needed no journalistic embroidery to enhance its drama.

The year 1930 brought another aeronautical sensation into the columns – this time a happy and successful one, as Hull's Amy Johnson, in her historic solo flight to Australia, not only brought credit to herself and her native city, but also advanced the progress of women into the world of technology. The *Hull Daily Mail,* by that time the City's only newspaper, having absorbed its last rival, the *Hull Evening News,* that very year, did 'Our Amy' proud, with page after page of stories and pictures.

In 1939, the darkness descended again. Britain was to be at war for the next six years, and by the end of that time, Hull was barely recognisable. Air raids were numerous throughout, but at first the damage was sporadic. Then, in May 1941, Hitler's bombers came in force, and, in two nights of 'Blitzkrieg,' tore the heart out of the city. Unlike Coventry and London, the port could not, for security reasons, share its agony with the world and receive due sympathy, being designated in the news bulletins 'a North-East Coast Town'.

But the *Hull Daily Mail* survived, and, with windows blown out and rubble littering the floors, its journalists and machine operators, many heavy-eyed from fire-watching the night before, recorded all the facts that it was permissible to print in those dangerous days.

Rebuilding – success and failure

When peace brought a relaxation of security, the story of the Blitz was told more fully by the *Hull Daily Mail's* former Assistant Editor, Tom Geraghty, in a booklet which was widely acclaimed and which enjoyed a second wave of success when it was re-printed by Hull Corporation a few years ago. The rebuilding of the City was slow and piecemeal. For weeks, the columns of the newspaper were filled with reports on the Abercrombie Plan, reluctantly abandoned because of the cost, and because it would have meant demolishing a number of viable buildings – including the *Hull Daily Mail's* Jameson Street offices.

Though there were some who condemned the City Fathers as faint-hearted at the time, there is little doubt that, had they yielded to the pleas of the idealists of the 1950's, razed the city centre to the ground and re-built to the Master's design, they would today have been condemned as vandals by the preservationists, who now prize many of the buildings which would have been swept away on the tidal wave of postwar town planning.

Honouring Amy Johnson, 1930

Much planning also went into the clearing of slum-dwellings and bomb-damaged homes and the building of new perimeter estates, together with the satellite town of Bransholme, between the villages of Sutton and Wawne.

Only qualified success in this endeavour could be recorded in the columns, however. 'Pram-parades' from slum to Guildhall, with placards proclaiming that 'the long-tails' (local word for rats, which it was unlucky to name in a seafaring community) were 'running over the bairns in the night', and that fungus was growing on the walls, were succeeded by complaints of social isolation in the new estates, of the splitting up of family and community.

In an attempt to re-create the mateyness of the old terraces, the planners built blocks of maisonettes with communicating balconies, quickly christened 'Alcatraz" and 'Colditz' by the residents, who discovered that living cheek-by-jowl with strangers and their often-undisciplined offspring was a far cry from life in the old communities of friends and relatives which had evolved naturally in the good old, bad old days of shared poverty and warm comradeship, when one could, with impunity, clip the ear of one's neighbour's kid as well as that of one's own. Besides, the maisonettes were later found to have severe structural faults, in common with similar ones in other Northern cities.

Until the 'Cod War' with Iceland and the EEC regulations virtually ended the fishing industry, an all-too-regular assignment for the *Hull Daily Mail's* editorial team, especially in the winter months, was the coverage of stories involving trawler losses, the worst coming in 1968, when the *St Romanus, Kingston Peridot* and *Ross Cleveland* sank within two weeks of each other, with the loss of all hands – save one. The incredible tale of the survival of Harry Eddom was the stuff of which the Norse Sagas were made.

Those who criticise newspaper reporters for intruding into the lives of the bereaved at these times certainly do not know the character of communities such as that which used to thrive on and around Hessle Road, the heart of the now fast-vanishing fishing industry. When tragedy struck, neighbours and friends rallied round, and one of those friends was the local newspaperman. His interest and sympathy was an important part of that back-up support which helped the family sustain their loss. His knock on the door and gentle opening: 'The Editor has sent me to express his sympathy...' was almost invariably greeted with a ready, 'Come in, lad. Hey, Mother, where's that picture of our Tom?' The treasured snap would be reached down from behind the pottery Alsatian on the mantelpiece by Mother, who, wiping her eyes on her apron, would reply, 'Here it is love – we knew the mister from the *Hull Daily Mail* would be coming.'

Folk culture preserved

These sea tragedies, which robbed the stricken families of a 'proper funeral' and a focal point where the flowers of mourning could be laid, probably account for the phenomenal survival, unique to the *Hull Daily Mail,* of the custom of placing numerous notices from friends, relatives, drinking pals and even, sometimes, to the embarrassment of wives and girl-friends, 'ladies of' the town', in the Deaths column, often accompanied by sentimental but sincerely meant tributes in verse and prose.

Staff are often asked whether mourners placing these notices are supplied with a book from which to select them. A list of suggestions, incorporating some of the more popular, is available, but it is only produced on request. Most notices are brought in by the clients themselves, and they are allowed considerable freedom in the wording of their own tributes.

The Deaths column and its adjacent sections for memorial notices and birthday remembrances serve as a kind of Garden of Remembrance for people whose loved ones have no known graves. Some people may laugh – and educationists occasionally wax very angry over this – but those who understand human nature and social history realise that here, in the advertisement columns of a local newspaper, a precious little piece of folk culture from the past is being kept alive, spontaneously, by the readers themselves, with the journal simply acting as an enabling medium.

The summer of 1961 produced a unique example of the influence and usefulness of a local newspaper in promoting public welfare. An outbreak of poliomyelitis brought into use, for the first time in this country, the new Salk vaccine, administered with great simplicity by placing a few drops on a lump of sugar.

At a few minutes before 5 pm on the day in question, the News Editor, Charles Levitt, received word from the Medical Officer of Health, Dr Alexander Hutchison, that the vaccine had arrived and that the clinics would be opened for its administration at five o'clock that evening.

Line by line, as the news was received, the story was typed out by Mr Levitt and dispatched through the sub-editors' room to catch the next edition, which came out about half-an-hour later. When he left the office with a colleague that afternoon, Mr Levitt drove to one of the clinics, housed in the old Nautical College in the Boulevard. As he turned the corner, a fantastic sight met his eyes. The queue waiting patiently outside was at least 200 yards long and five deep. All the evening, until the clinic ran out of vaccine at about 9 pm, the queue never grew less – and the scene was being repeated at other clinics all over the City. People came from as far as Scarborough for their sugar-lumps, and, by the end of the campaign, a larger number of people had been immunised than the whole population of Hull – about 375,000 in all. At that time, the *Hull Daily Mail* was the only source of local news, and its role in controlling the outbreak cannot be over-estimated.

During the 1970's, many important stories hit the headlines. The opening of communications through the M62 motorway and link roads meant that the City's relative freedom from 'big' crime was at an end.

But this did not account for some of the more sensational murders of the decade, the infamous Bruce Lee case – a series of deliberate fire-raisings believed to have killed no fewer than 26 people, including the three Hastie children and 11 old men resident in the Wensley Lodge home for the elderly at Hessle – undoubtedly ranking as the most macabre. Lee, a mentally disturbed youth with a declared ambition to make the *Guinness Book of Records*, was later, after much parliamentary questioning and re-examination of the evidence, given the benefit of the doubt over several of the cases, including the Wensley Lodge tragedy, but he continues to be detained in a top security hospital.

Though not so startling in its impact, the story of the building and opening of the Humber Bridge, the largest single-span suspension bridge in the world, must, however, stand as one of the newspaper's most important recent assignments in terms of living history recorded for generations to come. The arguments, the long delays, the labour squabbles, the near-disaster as one section broke away – how to report these in readable style, holding the public's interest and not satiating it with too much detail, was a continuing challenge for a succession of editors, news editors and picture editors. But there was beauty there, too, to be pictured and described – beauty and strength and ingenuity, and the dogged faith, courage and tenacity of those for whom the rising structure was the fulfilment of a dream, not only of a magnificent piece of engineering but of a link which would unite the North and South Banks, making Humberside a reality.

The Falklands Campaign of 1982 brought another challenge, for many Hull men – and ships, including the North Sea Ferries vessel, *Norland,* and a number of trawlers – were involved, and during the spring and summer of that year the newspaper was crammed with dramatic stories of courage and daring, followed by accounts of the pride and thankfulness with which Humberside welcomed those who returned safely home.

Facts, fun and features

Aside from its news coverage, a newspaper must, if it is to hold its readership, also offer a reasonable service of factual information, embracing such things as weather forecasts, lighting-up times, market prices, radio and TV programmes, sports results and a host of similar items. Into the category of 'information' come also its advertisement services – but more of that later. More, too, will be said of sports coverage, which must surely head the list of services provided under the general heading of 'Entertainment'. Latterly, the popular 'Find the Ball' and Bingo games were introduced, together with a host of competitions and other features.

Cultural endeavours must similarly be recognised. Music, art, exhibitions, and the theatre and cinema, both amateur and professional, all have to be found a place in the pages, along with items of special interest to women, dress patterns and cookery hints, a children's feature maybe, a crossword puzzle, bridge and chess brain-teasers, and a cartoon to make the reader laugh – or think!

Over the decades, the *Hull Daily Mail's* copious and strongly-political editorials gradually shrank, lost their party bias, and, under the editorship of Bill Sneyd, disappeared altogether. But that did not mean that the newspaper became a rudderless barge, drifting on the tide of events, simply recording them without fire or passion. On the contrary, it seemed to enable the paper's roots to sink further into the soil of Hull. The readers' letters feature, always a strong and much-read part of the journal, was extended, and here the cut-and-thrust of viewpoint and debate continued between named protagonists, gaining renewed vigour.

At the same time, the daily 'Diary' columnists, John Humber and Jane Humber, were given a free hand to lace their staple copy-diet of stories and paragraphs about people and events with comment on controversial topics – but only as when they felt inspired to do so, and not under the obligation of having to produce a specific number of centimetres in this vein each day. These sallies were often answered by readers, supporting or condemning the views expressed. Thus, in place of' an anonymous leader writer, whose origins might be many miles away, the *Hull Daily Mail* offered gut-reactions from local people living and working in the community, and well known as personalities in their own right.

With the change-over in the 1970's from the hot metal system of production to the slower but more streamlined photoset method, and co-incidental with the development of local radio and television, the *Hull Daily Mail* began augmenting its news coverage with more in-depth features, requiring detailed research by specialist staff. These features highlighted Humberside's services and institutions, probed problems such as teenage drug-taking and glue-sniffing, alcoholism and lawlessness, homelessness among young families, the integration of the Vietnamese Boat People, the care of the aged, or divorce and the rising numbers of children going into care, and focused on the strengths and weaknesses of the County's medical, social and educational provisions, or took a look inside the City's top security jail.

Thus, Hull's local newspaper continues to seek and find news stories, to inform, to entertain, to nag a little ... and to show that it cares.

Zeppelin damage in the Old Town resulting from a raid on 6 June 1915.

The opening of the Humber Bridge.

The Formula Was Right

In 1885, a group of Hull businessmen took over an old-fashioned Conservative weekly newspaper and transformed it into a bright new daily. Their object, it was widely believed, was to put one of their number, Frederick Brent Grotrian, into Parliament.

That object achieved a year later, why did the paper not then, or at some subsequent time, join the scores of others up and down the country which had come into being to bang a political or other propaganda drum, and had vanished as soon as they had served their purpose? The germ of the answer may lie in an often-quoted extract from the first edition of the paper, published from 22 Whitefriargate on September 29, 1885, in which an editorial frankly stated that 'it did not pretend that the *Hull Daily Mail* is established otherwise than as a commercial and dividend-earning venture'.

'We have no philanthropic object in view which will lead us to expound crochets at a pecuniary loss to ourselves, and at a loss to the temper of our readers,' the leader writer declared. The aim from the first, then, was to turn out a sellable product, which the people would want to buy and would read with both enjoyment and profit.

This policy may have been shaped by F. B. Grotrian himself. London-born and educated, but 'a Hull man in everything but birth', he had made a name for himself in the city as an astute businessman, but one with a heart. 'His Conservatism was leavened and tempered by Liberal tendencies,' said one of the tributes written after his death in 1905. 'It was never the hard, rigid unprogressive and unproductive type. 'Political power had been given to the masses, and the Conservative Party, if they were to lead and influence the people, had to adjust itself to new and inevitable conditions.' Among his many friends in his East Hull election fights were working men. 'Many of them proved loyal to him in a manner and to an extent that never left his memory, and it is not too much to claim that he was as staunch in his loyalty to them. He always spoke of them with gratitude and sincere respect.' Though he represented East Hull in Parliament for only six years, Mr Grotrian never forgot the people of his constituency, and later, when times were hard, he sent large sums of money for relief work among the needy, the source of this benevolence being revealed only after his death.

Such a man might well have laid down an editorial policy which ensured that, while the leading articles might pipe the Party tune, no liberties were to be taken with the accuracy and impartiality of the news reporting, and that the citizens who invested their halfpennies in the new evening journal should get their money's worth. 'Latest telegrams, local and commercial news. Special sporting news,' promised a handbill sent out in advance of the launching.

Whoever was responsible for the planning, however, the formula was right; and through changes of ownership, editorship and management, the *Hull Daily Mail* seems to have gone on giving the readers what they wanted over the past 100 years. Whether by luck or a succession of coincidental good judgments, the paper has always contrived to maintain a recognisable identity, appealing to the majority of the local population as 'the friend that comes through the letterbox'.

A silver snuff-box

According to the historian, Sheahan, the first newspaper published in Hull was the *Courant*, printed in Lowgate in 1759 and bearing the imprint of Rawson and Sons.

The *Hull Packet* made its first appearance on May 29, 1787. It had four pages, each eight columns wide, and sold at 7d – a lot of money in those days. So, in common with most newspapers then, it was not for the ordinary working man, who probably could not read, anyway. It was printed by Ann Prince in 1790 – an early example, perhaps, of feminine participation in business – and was later published by Robert Peck and printed in Scale Lane, Hull, by George Prince, suggesting that Ann's involvement may have come about through family connections, or marriage. In November, 1827, the paper was bought by a Mr Allanson, who enlarged it and re-titled it, *Hull Packet and Humber Mercury.* It was then being printed and published by T. Topping, of Lowgate. In 1830, Mr Topping sold out to Goddard and Brown, who were the publishers until 1839.

During the year which preceded the passing of the Reform Bill of 1832, giving wider franchise to the people, especially those of the Northern towns created or enlarged by the Industrial Revolution, Mr S. C. Hall, a Fellow of the Society of Arts, wrote the leading articles for the *Packet*, and his success in putting the message across may be inferred from the fact that, when he left, the proprietors presented him with an inscribed silver snuff-box. Mr. Brown continued to publish the paper after his partnership with Mr Goddard had been dissolved, taking on Mr Andrew Clarke Wardale as a partner, and with a Mr Quinn, or Queen, as editor. Shortly afterwards, however, Mr Q left the *Packet* to work for Mr Goddard, who had started an opposition paper on Conservative principles entitled *The Hull and East Riding Times.* Its life was short, however, and in 1841 it ceased to exist.

The same year, Mr Brown relinquished his ownership of the *Packet*, and in 1842 it was sold to Mr Thomas Freebody, who was acting for a group of leading Conservatives in Hull and district. The editor at that time was Mr T. Ramsey, author of a novel entitled *Ponsonby.* Mr Ramsey, however, was later to lose his job because of his religious convictions. This was the time of the Puseyite controversy, a reference to Dr E. B. Pusey (1800-1890), one of a group of university dons who, in the mid-19th century, founded the Oxford Movement. This had a strong political element, for it was designed to restore the autonomy of the Church of England, freeing it from control by Parliament and also bringing back the traditional rituals. Its adherents, variously known as 'Tractarians' or 'Puseyites', or, at a later stage, 'Ritualists' and 'Anglo-Catholics', believed that the Anglican Church was the successor in England of the 'primitive Church'. As Mr Ramsey was a High Church man, his views ran counter to those of his employers, and in 1845 he gave way to his sub-editor, who bore the splendidly Dickensian name of Dibdin Hubbarde. It

Early newspapers, The Hull Packet *and* The Rockingham; *(bottom right) the* Hull Daily Mail's *original premises at 22 Whitefriargate.*

The Hull Daily Mail

AND EAST YORKSHIRE AND LINCOLNSHIRE COURIER.

(WITH WHICH IS INCORPORATED THE HULL AND LINCOLNSHIRE TIMES.)

NO. 1.   [REGISTERED FOR TRANSMISSION ABROAD]   **TUESDAY, SEPTEMBER 29, 1885.**   ONE HALFPENNY.

AMUSEMENTS AND NOTICES.

SALES BY AUCTION.

IN COMPETITION WITH THE WORLD.

The front page of the first Hull Daily Mail **in 1885.**

seems strange in these sceptical days, when even the highest of churches appear to adopt a fairly pragmatic attitude, that a man should be prepared to lay down his job for his conscience. But the Puseyites evidently believed sincerely that a divine leadership had passed from Rome to the Anglican Church after the Reformation, and that this transcended the man-made laws of Westminster.

★ ★ ★ ★

Mr Hubbarde kept the editorial seat warm for only a matter of months, however, being succeeded the same year by Mr Richard Wallis, who had joined the paper in 1845 as Chief Reporter, and he still held the editorship when Sheahan published his *History* in 1866, describing the *Packet* as 'the oldest Hull newspaper in existence and the only Conservative and Church paper between Hull and York'. Meanwhile, in 1849, Mr Wallis had taken over as manager and publisher as well as editor, and in 1856, along with his elder brother, Ebenezer Wallis, he bought the paper. In 1857, the brothers added a penny Saturday journal called *The Hull and North Lincolnshire Times*. The *Packet* continued until September, 1885, when it was bought and absorbed by the *Hull Daily Mail*.

The Night they Took Umbrage
The 19th century was a time of great growth in public literacy. Long before the Education Act of 1870 began producing new literates from among the poorest classes, the reformers had been at work, chipping away at the restrictions on newspapers – the so-called 'taxes on knowledge'. 'The political liberation of the Press was completed in 1855 by the repeal of the stamp duty on newspapers and crowned in 1862 by the repeal of the paper duty,' recorded William Hunt, founder editor of the *Eastern Morning News*, in his account of his 50 years in journalism, *Then and Now*.

The development of machinery to speed up printing, and the opening up of rail services to take the end product to its many destinations also played their parts in the expanding newspaper industry, as did the increasing efficiency of the telegraph, the setting up of international newsagencies such as Reuters, and the formation, just over 100 years ago by a group of provincial newspaper proprietors, of the Press Association.

Newspapers cheapened and multiplied, springing up everywhere; weeklies were transformed into dailies. In his *History of Hull Newspapers*, Mr R. A. Brewer, former Chief Sub-Editor of the *Hull Daily Mail* and, after that, its 'John Humber' columnist, traced no fewer than 28 different papers which began in Hull, and ran for varying times during the 19th century. With the addition of their associated weeklies, the number of titles was around 35, but only two groups, the *Hull Daily Mail* and the *Eastern Morning News*, survived into the present century. *The Eastern Morning News*, which began publication on January 26, 1864, was not the first daily to appear in Hull. That distinction belongs to the *Hull Morning Telegraph*, which was started in 1855 to report the daily progress of the Crimean War, and which evidently outlived its original purpose for quite some time by building up a strong advertising service.

★ ★ ★ ★

Before leaving the history of the *Hull Packet*, it might be amusing to recall a joke played on its editorial team by a former member of its staff, T. Dennis Kendall, who had gone over to the new *Eastern Morning News* as its first Assistant Editor.

Because of his earlier association with the *Packet*, he knew how late news was dealt with there, and one night, egged on by one of his waggish friends at the White Hart Inn, young Dennis, who evidently liked his tipple more than somewhat, contrived a message, rigged as though it had come from the telegraph office, which would reach the *Packet* either late on Thursday night or early on Friday morning, announcing under the heading 'War in Denmark', that the enemy had taken Umbrage. The bogus message went on to give the geographical location of 'Umbrage', placing it about the middle of the North Sea, and adding its population and other details.

The 'taking of Umbrage' was the talk of the town on the Friday and Saturday, but naturally the hoax caused Mr Richard Wallis really to take umbrage, and he wrote to Mr Hunt saying that the bogus message had been traced to the *Eastern Morning News* office.

Mr Hunt immediately sacked T. Dennis Kendall, who was duly caricatured in *Punch* as 'the hass that sends false news to the papers'. History does not record what happened to the *Packet* sub-editor who was taken in by the hoax, but evidently the incident did Kendall no permanent professional harm, as he later did well as the London correspondent of the *Scotsman*, and subsequently worked for the Press Association, though he died at an early age 'through dissipation'. Recalling the incident, Mr Brewer goes on to reflect that, during World War II, 'Lord Haw-Haw', the British renegade William Joyce, set the whole country laughing by solemnly announcing over the German radio that the British had admitted that the Forces of the Reich had captured Umbrage! It leaves one wondering just how old the joke really is . . .

An Inspired Partnership

The founders the Hull, East Yorkshire and North Lincolnshire Conservative Newspaper and Printing Co. Ltd comprised, in addition to Mr F. B. Grotrian, Sir A. K. Rollit, Col. A. K. Dibb, Mr S. R. Pease, Mr Mark Bean and Maj. C. Judge, all men of renown in the city. The editor and publisher was Mr George Eastwood of 7, All Saints Street, Hull. Though the new paper represented, in its day, the last word in bright modern journalism, its four modest pages, with advertisements covering the first and its news columns crowded with stories printed in small, close type and introduced by sober little headlines, were hardly eye-catching by today's standards.

Neither, however, was Lord Northcliffe's revolutionary new national newspaper, the *Daily Mail*, which made its appearance on May 4 eleven years later. This eight-page broadsheet announced as 'The busy man's daily journal' and 'A penny newspaper for one halfpenny', also had advertisements on the front page – though some of them were among the most entertaining items in the paper:

'Uncle Jim – Come home at once. All is forgiven. Bring the pawn tickets with you.'

'Will the gentleman who took away by mistake the Brown Pony standing outside the Star and Garter on City and Suburban Day, kindly send to the same place for the trap, or return pony? The one is no use without the other.'

One might be forgiven for suspecting that these were the inventions of some of the editorial staff! Picture coverage, apart from two little fashion sketches, was nil, despite the claim that the paper was being produced by new machinery, 'on a scale unprecedented in any English newspaper office'.

Stories abound concerning the adoption by Northcliffe of the title, *Daily Mail*, but they are not very well documented. Hearsay has it that the proprietors of the London paper wrote to the *Hull Daily Mail* asking for permission to use the title, *Daily Mail*, and that this was given. Some add that at the time it was not thought feasible for a paper printed in London to be sold in Hull the same day – a feat soon made possible by improved rail services – and others suggest that at some stage there was some kind of litigation.

It seems likely that the matter of the title was examined by lawyers acting for both companies, and it is certainly true that around that time – 1896 – the Yorkshire paper's Gothic masthead, The *Hull Daily Mail*, with the words, *Hull Packet and East Yorkshire and Lincolnshire Courier* underneath, was replaced by the familiar, *The Daily Mail* in plain but distinctive lettering.

Too Many Cooks . . . ?

Launching a new paper in 1885 was an even more precarious venture than it is in this highly-competitive age. On the *Hull Daily Mail's* first anniversary, a celebration dinner was held at the Malt Shovel, North Church Side, where a message was read from Mr Grotrian acknowledging the anxiety of the employees to co-operate with the proprietors in bringing success to their enterprise. He knew, he said, that they realised it was no light undertaking and no small risk to make a new departure in journalism: 'The proprietors were anxious for the employees' welfare and well-being, and most desirous that their working conditions should be as comfortable as possible.'

The new paper, however, quickly won approbation – and from a fellow publication at that! Writing in the *Hull and East Riding Critic*, 'A Satirical and Independent Journal', editor Richard Cooke declared: 'A long-felt want has at last been supplied. The public of Hull have long needed a daily paper which would devote its columns to local news, and not to information about how the King of Siam's toothache was progressing and such like uninteresting pudding. The *Hull Daily Mail* has appeared upon the scene, and if it keeps up as it has commenced, we shall not have to buy the London *Daily Telegraph* or the *Newcastle Chronicle* to find out what is going on in the immediate vicinity of the Third Port, as we have had to do. The Mail's chief fault, that I can see, lies in its lack of quantity – not in its quality. I understand, however, that as soon as new machinery is ready, its size will be increased by four columns. Its articles and notes are smartly written, and every scribe on the staff appears as if he had instructions not to mince matters, but to call a spade a spade.'

* * * *

Little is on record concerning the paper's first editor, George Eastwood, and only a brief curriculum vitae is available covering its second editor, who bore the somewhat unusual name of Henry Joy Corlyon – could the surname have been a corruption of 'Coeur de Lion', and was there, perhaps, a Huguenot connection? Mr Corlyon had served his apprenticeship on the *Hull Packet*, starting in 1854. After several years there, he joined the *Eastern Morning News*, and while still a very young man, moved on to London, where he represented the Central News press agency in the gallery of the House of Commons. He returned to Hull to become Chief Reporter of the *Eastern Morning News* and *Hull Express*, resigning this appointment to take up his editorship with the *Hull Daily Mail*. But later he returned once more to the *Eastern Morning News* this time as editor.

Mr Brewer records that a paper called the *Hull Globe*, published by N. Waller and H. J. Corlyon at 56, Lowgate, existed in 1888, so Henry evidently had fingers in other newspaper pies as well.

His son, Billy Corlyon, was Chief Reporter of the *Hull Daily Mail* for many years, during which time he built up a record of events which became a kind of 'bible' in the newspaper's library. Billy, who eventually became a well-known Hull publican, covered most of the big local stories of his day, and on one occasion, when King Edward VII was ill, Billy had the temerity to telephone Buckingham Palace for news. 'To his surprise, he was most courteously answered, and the *Hull Daily Mail* printed the latest bulletin several hours before it was posted outside Buckingham Palace walls for the pressmen to copy,' says an account of the incident.

* * * *

The newspaper's early years were by no means free from trouble, however. Perhaps it was a case of 'too many cooks . . .' At all events, it is recorded that, when Frederick Brent Grotrian bought out his fellow directors in 1890 and decided to run the show himself, 'new drive was infused into the organisation'. One of the first things he did was to appoint Edgar Samuel Lewis as editor-manager, giving him a free hand. With wide editorial experience behind him in other parts of the country, Lewis brought a new and vigorous era to Hull journalism. 'A forceful and original writer, he adopted the then farsighted policy of giving all sides, creeds and parties a fair share of *Hull Daily Mail* space – not always to the liking of certain interests in those days,' says an article in the newspaper's archives.

Those were the days when newspapers often actively participated in local and national affairs, and Mr Lewis played a dramatic role in the great dock strike which broke out in 1893. The incident which sparked it off happened aboard the *Ariosta*, the Wilson Line's Gothenburg butter boat lying in Albert Dock. The reckless discharge of a firearm by a London stevedore caused the first disorder, and from then on the dispute escalated.

'I was present when the Hull dockers charged the "blacklegs" and for six weeks, night and day, was seldom off the dock,' Chief Reporter Billy Corlyon recorded in his memoirs. Mr Lewis interviewed Ben Tillett and other dockers' leaders, and his initiative contributed greatly to the settlement of the dispute.

Described as 'an inspired partnership', proprietor and editor collaborated in more than one crusade. The North Eastern Railway's monopoly and Hull's fight to preserve its foreshore rights were among their joint interests – and, if their lead to rid Hull of its level-crossings did not bring success, it was a measure of the magnitude of a problem which was to plague the City for at least another half-century, rather than any lack of vigour on their part!

The *Hull Daily Mail's* influence was never more firmly felt than when the City itself was poised for a great advance. Hull was crippled at that time by an unsympathetic railway monopoly and inadequate dock facilities, and merchants and ship-owners rose against the unequal burden. Mr. Grotrian was the chief protagonist, and was one of three guarantors for the promotion in Parliament of a Bill to construct a tunnel under the Humber, connecting with the Manchester, Sheffield and Lincolnshire railway at Brigg and Appleby to give access to the south and west. The Bill was, however, rejected by the House of Lords Committee, who were not happy about the engineering details.

'The defeat of the Hull and South West Junction Bill was probably the greatest public blow Mr Grotrian ever received. The work in connection with this important scheme and the disappointment it inflicted nearly cost him his life,' wrote his biographer.

When Frederick Brent Grotrian died at Ingmanthorpe Hall, Wetherby, in 1905, a private company was formed to run the newspaper, the board consisting of his four sons, Mr (later Sir) H. Brent Grotrian, KC, MP, who was chairman; Mr Fred Grotrian; Mr Edgar Grotrian, who took over as managing director; and Maj. H. H. Grotrian, together with Mr Lewis, who completed a total of 32 years of editorship before his death in Torquay in 1922. The Lewis involvement with the newspaper was also a family affair. Edgar's wife was the *Hull Daily Mail's* first 'lady contributor', starting the column, 'House and Home' under the nom-de-plume of 'Mother Humber' and founding, in 1907-8, her well-known 'coal and distress fund', which was to continue after her death as the Mother Humber Memorial Fund. Their son, Mr Edgar Wills Lewis, succeeded his father as editor; and another member of the family, Mr E. E. Lewis, held a post described as that of Special Commissioner, or overseas representative.

Advancing Technology

The year 1885, which saw the birth of the *Hull Daily Mail,* was also the year in which an American immigrant watchmaker, Otto Mergenthaler, aided by engineer James O. Clephane, patented the Linotype machine. This was to revolutionise typesetting, being superseded only by the advent of photosetting techniques nearly 100 years later.

It was not until 1897 that the *Hull Daily Mail* took delivery of its first Linotype, but long before that, and shortly after the Grotrian-Lewis partnership had been cemented, stereo plant was installed, enabling the lumbering Wharfedale flat-bed printing press, with its 1,500 copies an hour top capacity, to be replaced by a rotary press capable at producing 8,000 copies in the same time.

This, too, quickly became obsolete and unable to cope with the demands of the rapidly-expanding *Hull Daily Mail,* and the weekly *Times* Series which it had acquired. On January 6, 1896, 'a large number of gentlemen' assembled at the Whitefriargate office to see the Mayors of Hull and Grimsby start a new and powerful press, together with two horizontal high-pressure engines, built by Marshalls of Gainsborough.

A second Hoe press was added, replacing a Victory press, and later still the two Hoes were supplemented by a third and much larger press in two parts, called a 'Quad'. These proved adequate until 1911, when, despite the extensions which had enlarged the Whitefriargate premises to at least four times their original area, 'a notable and costly addition' to the mechanical equipment was rendered necessary by 'the ever-increasing demands of readers and by the ever-growing extension of the advertising connection in London and in Yorkshire of the new newspapers published from these offices.'

This addition was a new three-roll press which would replace a smaller one, and would produce 4, 6, 8, 10 or 12-page papers at the rate of 33,000 per hour, double the rate of the press that had been displaced. 'The new press is one of the best that the well-known English and American firm of Hoe and Company are turning out, and it is in all respects an English-made machine,' proclaimed a booklet issued to commemorate the event.

At the same time, new foundry equipment was installed to facilitate the casting of stereo plates from the impressions taken on papier-mache sheets, or 'flongs', as they were known, of the made-up pages in the composing room. 'It consists of an improved metal pot and patent pump, two casting boxes and planing machine, all electrically driven,' says the booklet. 'The new metal pot is fitted with a pump, and, instead of the old system of ladling out metal by hand into the casting boxes, the metal is now pumped into casting boxes placed up against the pot. A spout is pulled into position, and the metal is pumped into the box and a plate made. Each of the boxes is fitted with a separate motor-driven saw to cut off the tail-piece of the plate; the page (or plate) is taken from the casting box, placed in the boring box, and a 6 hp motor soon runs over the inside of the plate, which is then ready for placing upon the printing machine.'

The system continued to operate in much the same way, give or take such details as the replacement of the papier-maché flong by a plastic one, for the next 60 years, until replaced by the modern Letterflex method.

Everything in Duplicate

In 1912, the composing department was described as 'a large and airy building specially adapted to its present use'. It was lighted in duplicate by gas and electricity and had a system of ventilation by air shafts and electrically-driven fans which placed it in the forefront of modern newspaper offices. The system of operating the machines, also in duplicate, was by electric motor direct to the mechanism.

The 'Comps' was in communication with all other departments by a system of house telephones. There were 14 Linotype machines, and here, too, was kept the Exchange Telegraph tape machine by means of which late news, racing, cricket, football and other results were received and, by a system of chutes, 'conveyed instantly to the printing machines in the basement'. Successors to this machine were in use in the Composing Room up to the 1970's.

Communication between composing and machine rooms was achieved in much the same way as that between the bridge and engine room of a ship, by means of a large dial which warned the printing and publishing departments of the arrival of important scores or other information. Specially designed 'fudge' boxes were sent flying down from the composing-room in little wheeled trucks, slotting straight into the press to print the 'late news' ... and so it was to continue until the photoset revolution of the 1970's.

Newspapers had begun to use illustrations from about 1890, and, three years later, Max Levy perfected the ruled half-tone screen which was to improve the reproduction of photographs on newsprint; but although the *Hull Daily Mail* kept up with the progress of picture coverage, it was not until after the move to Jameson Street in 1926 that it installed its own process engraving department for the production of picture blocks.

In 1912, the *Hull Daily Mail*, *Hull and East Yorkshire Times* and *Hull and Lincolnshire Times* were all being produced from 22, Whitefriargate; and the following year they were joined by the *Sports Mail*.

'It can be claimed fairly that the *Mail* and *Hull Times* appeal to every interest and section in a thriving commercial and shipping community,' declared the 1912 booklet. 'Apart from the best general news features, there are regular series of articles and notes devoted every week to specific pursuits and sports. Women are catered for by "Mother Humber's" weekly letter, "House and Home", which has been established 21 years. Patriotic duty is studied in Territorial Notes and Rifle Shooting Notes. Football is dealt with to the average extent of 20 columns in the course of a week, and the *Mail* and *Times* also have their own representative travelling with the Yorkshire Cricket Team. There is a weekly golf column, and bowls, angling, chess, whist and billiards are discussed by experts. In the realm of public affairs, there is a weekly Labour Letter, and frequent communications from the Colonies, where there are a large number of Hull and East Yorkshire and Lincolnshire families. Answers to correspondents, gardening notes, farmer's letter, church notes, 'Round the Town' etc, are included weekly in the *Hull Times*. The *Mail* is an unrivalled local medium for public discussion. Its correspondence columns are crowded with letters from readers on questions of the day, a proof at once of healthy public opinion and the popularity of the medium through which it is expressed. The *Mail* can conscientiously claim to have influenced great movements for the progress of Hull and its neighbourhood, and it has been actuated by public spirit and independence of the cramping, sectional limits which often restrict the usefulness and progress of a newspaper.'

The company was proud, too, of its record in the raising of public subscriptions for 'patriotic and charitable objects', a list of which throws quite a revealing light on the social conditions of the day: The Distillery Disaster Fund, 1898 (£43.18); the Bullfinch Disaster Fund, 1899 (£25); the Bedford Street Fire Fund, 1901 (£81); the Hungry Schoolchildren's Fund, 1904 (£502); the Boer War Fund, 1900 (over £1,000); the Mother Humber Fund, 1907-11 (over £1,400); and the 'Bootless Bairns Fund', 1909 (£312).

The *Hull Times* also began issuing, in 1911, Long Service Medals, which were awarded to workers in the district who had given continuous service to an employer for a minimum of 25 years – and these medals still turn up occasionally at spring-cleaning time in local households!

Hull's 'Little Fleet Street'

The year of 1914 was a momentous one for Hull – and, of course, for the country as a whole. The Humber port, however, was to remember it as the year in which it acquired a fine new dock – and a Lord Mayor. On June 26, King George V, accompanied by Queen Mary, came to Hull to open the dock which bears his name, and, the ceremony concluded, the King bestowed upon the city's Chief Citizen, Alderman John Henry Hargreaves, the title of Lord Mayor. The *Hull Daily Mail* commemorated the occasion with a 24-page Royal number, quite a mechanical feat in those days. The issue contained a detailed report of all the events of the day, including speeches at the luncheon, and carried more than 100 columns of advertisements. The revenue from the latter probably accounted for the fact that the price was still only a halfpenny.

Former Composing Room Overseer Harold Wright, who started an apprenticeship with the newspaper in 1915, following his father into the business, recalls that it was in 1914 that the first regular 24-page papers were published: 'Because the presses could not take a 24, it was decided to print two 12's with a blue seal on Pages 1 and 15 and the Stop Press on Pages 12 and 24. This was all right until it was learned that the paper boys had charged for each paper!' he said. Another of Mr Wright's reminiscences of the Whitefriargate days concerned the publication during the racing season of a daily sheet called *The Flash*. It was printed on both sides with the flat races of the day, adding details of form, probable runners and jockeys, and tips. It was published for some years, but was withdrawn following strong opposition from the rival 'Sporting Pink'.

By the autumn of 1914, the nation was at war, but gloom and doom were not apparent. Many of the younger folk, innocent of the grim realities, quite welcomed the notion of a scrap with Kaiser Bill – and it was all going to be over by Christmas, anyway… The *Hull Daily Mail* announced that it was suspending Mother Humber's weekly column 'during the crucial weeks of the war'. Little did anyone suspect what was to follow – the shortages of food and other commodities, the bombs raining down on helpless civilians from Count Von Zeppelin's monstrous dirigibles, and the ghastly losses at the front, culminating in the carnage of Oppy Wood, which claimed the flower of Hull's young manhood. Peace came eventually, however, and the nation was soon whooping it up in the Roaring Twenties, trying to forget both the horrors of the past and the economic difficulties of the present, then so unequally shared across the social strata.

Whitefriargate was quite a 'little Fleet Street' in those days, with the *Eastern Morning News, Hull Evening News* and weekly *Hull News* all operating under the same umbrella on the north side and the *Hull Daily Mail* and its own group of weeklies on the south.

The *Eastern Morning News*, as has already been said, was established in 1864, and around 1884 the *Hull Daily News*, an evening paper, entered the field in the Liberal interest and in direct opposition to the *Mail*. 'While it came some distance behind in the matter of popularity and circulation, it contested the ground rigorously,' we are told. In 1912, the paper's title was changed to the *Hull Evening News*.

Competition was fierce, especially in the matter of being first with the sports results, vociferously proclaimed by the street sellers in and around Victoria Square. Harold Wright recalled that, when the *Hull Daily Mail* pipped the opposition to the post, the normally reserved and scholarly editor, Edgar Wills Lewis, would clap him on the shoulder and exclaim, 'We beat 'em, Harold – we beat 'em!' And the one-time editor of the *Eastern Morning News*, Mark Goulden, who later achieved distinction in the publishing and film business, opened his autobiography, *Mark My Words*, with an account of how he scooped the field with the first news of the R38 disaster, which he had witnessed – along with most of the population of Hull – as he was leaving his office. The *Hull Daily Mail*, however, was not far behind in rushing out a special edition on the happening. Special editions were thick and heavy before the advent of radio.

Features proliferated in the 1920's too; there were news stories of all kinds, columns of information on concerts, the magic names of Heifetz and Clara Butt hitting the headlines, theatrical reviews and, of course, a crescendo of comment on the booming cinematograph.

Unloading paper in West Street at the rear of the Jameson Street premises in a way which Health and Safety would never allow today.

In Jameson Street

By the middle of the decade, the Whitefriargate offices were bursting at the seams. Despite the laudatory terms in which the modernisation had been described in 1912, the building itself was an old one, and Harold Wright recalled that, even when he started there as a boy, some of the departments presented a somewhat Heath Robinson appearance. One of the presses was housed in a 'buoy shed' which had belonged to the *Hull Daily Mail's* landlords, Hull Trinity House, which owns most of the property on that side of the street, and the insertion of a reel of newsprint into one machine involved crawling into a waterlogged pit underneath. If a compositor was unwise enough to leave his packet of sandwiches in the pocket of his coat when he hung it up, he was liable to find a rat nibbling at the contents when he went back for it. The Whitefriargate entrance gave on to an advertisement department and reception area only; to reach the main offices and works, one had to walk down Princes Dock Side and through an archway.

The directors took advantage of street improvements to acquire a site in the new Jameson Street, which was then under development. There, on a site bounded in the rear by West Street and South Street, the building of a block of offices began in 1925, to be opened the following year. In addition to the premises to be occupied by the newspaper, the property included several shops, together with a block of offices known as 'The Mail Buildings', originally all let off to business tenants, but later partly reclaimed to accommodate sections of the ever-expanding newspaper activities. 'The site had previously been covered by small, dilapidated properties, the clearance of which formed a great improvement to the aspect of the locality,' said a contemporary report.

'In years gone by, and not very remote either, any old building was considered good enough in which to print and publish a newspaper, but it is not so today, when the industry is one of the most important in the country,' wrote Managing Director Edgar Grotrian in a foreword to the handsomely-produced illustrated booklet issued to mark the opening. He went on: 'The provincial newspaper – covering such a great area as ours – has many duties and obligations to perform. It is a public institution, and part of the commercial and social structure. It embraces every popular interest and enters into the daily life of the people more than any other institution. It must deal accurately and impartially with all sides of life, in due proportion. It takes many years to build up and obtain the confidence so necessary for its success, but, once attained, there is between it and its readers a most intimate relationship, which would be difficult to efface – a relationship of goodwill, friendship and co-operation which survives all petty differences of opinion and recognises that in their efforts on behalf of the common weal, Press and Public are one.'

The Jameson Street premises, a building which inspired much loyalty but became inadequate for the increasing demands made on it.

The Structure of the Building

The site for the new buildings comprised 1,426 square yards with a frontage of 156 feet 6 inches to West Street, 88 feet 6 inches to South Street, and a shop frontage on the ground floor level to Jameson Street. The building comprised a basement, ground, first, second and third floors, with a mezzanine floor between the ground floor and first-floor level along the West Street frontage. The total height from pavement level was 55 feet 3 inches on the West Street frontage and 53 feet on the South Street frontage.

The ground was excavated over the whole area to the depth necessary for the provision of the basements required for the accommodation of the machine beds, motors, etc, under the full area of the machine department, the remainder being used for reserve stocks of newsprint, furnace rooms, ink stores and parking-places for employees' cycles. After the Second World War, the possession of this large basement area – one of the few in Hull free from the then-recurrent menace of flooding – proved a strong point in resisting the Abercrombie Plan, which would have meant the demolition of the building. The load of the building, concentrated at some 120 points, was supported on heavy pitch pine piles, sunk to a depth of 26 feet. Fire-resisting construction was adopted throughout, the whole of the floor and roof being made of hollow concrete slabs carried on a girder work of steel, which in turn was surrounded by concrete as a complete protection against fire.

The concrete floors were finished on top in wood blocks and tiles, in accordance with the requirements of the various departments, while the flat concrete roof was rendered impervious to moisture by a covering of asphalt. Central heating by means of a low-pressure hot water system, and a fully electric lighting installation further emphasised the up-to-the-minute aspect of the building. 'The external elevations are treated with due respect to the architectural dictum that a building should express in concrete form the purpose for which it is intended,' said the commemoration booklet. 'A frankly modern elevation, of modern materials, is blended in a direct manner into a dignified whole. A faience plinth, from seven to eleven feet in height, has been specially manufactured to a granite tone and finished with a glazed surface, ensuring the cleanliness of the building at street level. To the South Street elevation, colour is added in the form of a name sign in blue toned terra cotta, attracting attention to the building in a quiet, dignified manner and in aesthetic harmony with its surroundings.'

* * * *

The principal entrance from Jameson Street, surrounded by a black granite architrave and elevated by three marble steps, led, in those days, through 'stately revolving doors' directly into the public hall, which occupied an area of 1,190 square feet and was paved throughout with Reptonwood tiles. 'Its walls are enriched by a simple treatment of panelling executed in multi-coloured Dutch Delft tiles, while light is admitted by a glazed dome in subdued colouring, and three smaller ceiling lights similarly treated,' continued the 1926 description. 'Plaster enrichments to the ceiling lights and ceiling itself complete the scheme of architectural decoration.'

The Commercial Department covered a floor area of 2,950 feet, and communicated directly with the counter in the public hall, thereby creating 'an atmosphere conducive to business efficiency'. The floor was of polished wood blocks and a polished mahogany panelled dado surrounded the entire department, while 'all useless ornament is omitted and effect gained by a simple plaster frieze and coffered ceiling'. Mahogany panelled screens divided the department into separate sections for accountant, cashier, advertisement manager, canvassers, book-keepers and others. Access from the ground floor to the editorial and other departments on the upper floors was gained by means of a high-speed passenger lift, and there was also a staircase constructed of non-slip stone, with a wrought-iron balustrade and mahogany handrail, with a dado of Dutch tiling embellishing the wall.

Despite the many changes which have been made over the years, callers of the 1980's would have had no difficulty in recognising the public sections of the building from the basic features which still remained.

The editorial department, comprising 4,300 square feet, was on the first floor, along with the telegraph and telephone rooms, and here, too, Managing Director Edgar Grotrian had his own office, handsomely finished with polished oak floor, fumed oak panelled walls, plaster-enriched ceiling and specially constructed and glazed windows.' The back staircase, leading down directly into West Street, was originally constructed for the convenience of the reporters, to speed them on their way to their various assignments.

The Mighty Presses

The Composing Room, with the proof-readers' annexe, covered a total area of 5,235 feet, and was roughly in the form of a T. By this time, the newspaper owned a battery of 24 Linotype machines, several printing machines for general work, and a complete case of equipment for the composition of advertisements.

Special attention was paid to cleanliness and lighting when constructing the new building. The floor was covered with special interlocking hardwood board, ensuring a smooth and practically dustless floor. The walls were lined throughout and to their entire height with white glazed brickwork. North-light roof trusses occupied the major portion of the ceiling area, which itself was painted white, so that that the light was always at its maximum. An ingenious piece of architectural planning ensured that the whole floor area of the two arms of the T were free from supporting columns.

The whole ground floor area on the South Street side of the premises was occupied by the printing machines, covering an area of 3,915 feet. The machine room was equipped with the most modern printing presses of their day, consisting of four 4-deck single-width presses and one double-width press. These five presses, two Crabtrees, two Hoes and a Goss, could turn out more than 300,000 copies per hour of an eight-page paper, printed, folded, counted and delivered; or 150,000 copies per hour of a 10-, 12-, 16- or 24-page paper. The driving equipment and motors powering the presses were placed in the basement, immediately beneath them, and a powerful stand-by oil engine was kept in reserve in case of any breakdown in the power or lighting.

The flooring between the machines was formed of steel chequer plates three-eighths of an inch thick, carried on a lattice of rolled steel joists. Natural lighting was secured by large windows on the South Street and West Street fronts and from an internal area. As in the Composing Room, the walls were lined in white glazed bricks.

The Linotype Room at Jameson Street.

Composing the pages at Jameson Street.

An electric goods lift was installed, connecting the Machine Room with the paper store in the basement and with the Linotype Room above, and a steel inspection gallery round two sides of the huge chamber afforded an easy means of general supervision.

Mention of this gallery will bring back memories for hundreds of readers who visited the *Hull Daily Mail*, for it provided a fine vantage point for watching the presses in operation without interfering with the work of the operators. When first installed, the great roaring presses were one of the mechanical wonders of the City; and even with so many other technological marvels to claim their attention, from stereo-sound to Concorde, parents brought their children to South Street to hear those mighty voices thundering as they printed the news on mile after mile of spinning ribbons of newsprint.

★   ★   ★   ★

Adjacent to the Machine Room was the foundry, occupying an area of 1,050 square feet and equipped with two Junior Autoplate casting machines, one heated by fire and the other by gas, and capable of producing two plates a minute. There the modern Letterflex sheets were produced at much less cost in hard labour by a photo-electric process involving the use of Polymer plastic which was economically re-cycled.

The Publishing Department, with its subsidiary rooms for distribution of supplies, occupied an area of 2,710 square feet. Connected directly with the publishing room itself, over a metal-covered counter with metal grille, was the cash sales room, in which newsboys received their supplies. A conveyor-belt was installed to take the newspapers from the Machine Room to the Publishing Department, and there were additional packing rooms for the preparation of train and bus parcels. With shrinking public transport services, most newspapers were distributed by the *Hull Daily Mail's* own large fleet of vans.

The Upper Floors

On the second floor, and directly accessible from the principal staircase and passenger lift, was the Board Room. 'Dignity is imbued to this room by a polished oak floor, panelled walls in wainscot oak, lightly fumed, plaster-enriched ceiling and large, open-hearth fireplace,' said the 1926 description. An anteroom, treated in a more simple manner and communicating directly with the Board Room, was later occupied by a succession of General Managers.

The remainder of the second floor was divided into rooms allocated to the distribution of the 'Mother Humber' and other charitable funds, artists' rooms, file rooms and general offices. Later, many of these were to give place to a spacious staff canteen, which at one time doubled as a games room, until, with the coming of the photoset system, the Process Engraving Department vacated its quarters on the floor above, and the games equipment was moved there. The second floor also housed the photographic dark-rooms and finishing-rooms, together with the Library – a vital source of records and information.

In 1926, however, the third floor, covering 1,025 square feet, was occupied by photographic departments and a process block room – a kind of library for the filing of advertisements and other picture and lettering blocks. Here, too, were the staff rest room and a small works' staff dining room, communicating with the flat

Casting the stereotype (the printing plate).

concrete roof, 'which is available for use as a recreation area during meal breaks'. Later, a caretaker's flat was erected on the south-east corner of the third floor.

The premises, very advanced for their day, had a complete internal telephone system – Relay Autophones – and each department had an electric synchronising clock. Some of those clocks were still in good working order in the 1980's.

How the front page was made up.

Each reel contained five miles of paper.

From Dragon's Blood to VDU'S

The move to Jameson Street was in itself no mean feat. Harold Wright recalls that a hole had to be made in the Composing Room floor at the Whitefriargate office so that the machines could be lowered on to lorries; and, to ensure uninterrupted publication, the two buildings were run together during the transition period.

Some time after the move, the *Hull Daily Mail* established its own Process Engraving Department for the production of picture blocks. This was situated on the top floor of the building, mainly so that the fumes from the chemicals used in the process could be disposed of harmlessly. Process Engraving was a combination of two arts, the ancient one of etching and the much more recent one of photography. To start with, all pictures were re-photographed, enlarged or reduced to the required size to fit the column widths.

In the case of a black-and-white line drawing, the method used was much the same as in ordinary photography, but for the reproduction of a photograph, in which the picture was full of graded tones, it was necessary to introduce a mechanical ruling of some kind to retain the gradation. For this purpose, the half-tone screen was brought into use. This was composed of two sheets of glass with lines ruled at an angle of 45 degrees. These sheets of glass were sealed together with the lines crossing each other at right angles so that a mesh was formed. Screens were made in varying degrees of coarseness and fineness according to the type of work required, 55 and 65 lines to the inch being in general use for newspaper reproductions. The screen was fitted inside a camera at a distance from a sensitised plate which was adjusted according to whether the photograph was to be enlarged or reduced, and the screen had the effect of breaking up the photographic surface into a mass of opaque dots, each varying in size in relation to the light and shade of the original.

The negative produced was then printed on to a piece of sheet zinc which had been previously prepared with a sensitised coating capable of resisting the action of acid. The negative was squeezed tightly into contact with the sensitised zinc sheet and exposed to a powerful arc lamp, the light of which acted only on the clear part of the negative between each opaque dot, thus leaving the portion of the surface immediately behind the dot unexposed. The plate was then simply 'developed' in water, when the unexposed portions, being soluble, were dissolved, leaving clear zinc between the exposed part which, through the action of light, had been made adhesive to the zinc, thus producing the positive picture. Now the plate was subjected to a heating process to harden the remaining film covering each dot, rendering it acid-resistant. Then the plate was placed in an etching machine – in effect, an acid spray – and the portions between the covered dots were bitten away, leaving in relief those required for printing.

For the reproduction of line drawings, no screen was used in the re-photographing process. The zinc print, taken by arc light, was washed and etched in the same manner, but was next given a short etch in nitric acid, then rolled with an acid-resisting ink, dusted with a red powder known as 'Dragon's Blood', and heated. This was done to prevent 'under-etching', the eating away of the walls and sides of the lines in the illustration. The plate was then re-etched and the process repeated until the necessary depth was obtained. The parts of the plates not required to carry a printing surface were cut away by means of an electric drill or router, and the finished zinc plates, both line and half-tone, were then mounted on metal blocks which were machined to a thousandth part of an inch to ensure that the printing surface was 'type-high', 0.918 inches. The operation sounds incredibly complicated, but in fact the staff of the Process Department could move incredibly fast, too, producing finished plates for important stories in minutes.

After the Second World War, the head of the department, Mr George Gohl, went to America to study new techniques, and this heralded the start of a series of modifications designed to streamline the production of picture blocks. The 'Dragon's Blood' gave place to more up-to-date material, the cumbersome glass plates to film negatives, new heating cupboards replaced the old gas-burners, the acid-baths were up-dated and new electronic scanning engravers were given trials, though these were not a great success.

During the transition from hot metal to photosetting, the Process Department produced work on plastic sheeting known as 'Dicryl', but this quickly gave place to up-to-date machines incorporating laser technology to reproduce drawings and photographs as simple photographic prints, or 'bromides'. The only vestige of the old system still remaining is, of course, the screen of dots which is necessary to produce a solid surface to which the ink can adhere in order to transfer the image to the paper.

Mr M. H. Broughton was manager of the Process Department, and his deputy Mr C. Walden.

Skill and Daring

Following the introduction of the halftone process, the *Hull Daily Mail's* press photographers soon built up a reputation for skill, resourcefulness and, frequently, amazing courage and daring. They would brave smoke and flames to capture dramatic fire pictures or climb to dizzy heights and lean out at precarious angles to obtain a good shot.

At first, they had nothing to augment natural lighting except the flare of magnesium powder ignited by a flint spark. Even in the 1950's they were still using the old VN plate cameras with flash bulbs. But World War II had brought vast improvements in fast photographic emulsions, making it possible to get good results using film.

The first film-loaded cameras to be introduced in the newspaper's photographic department were the legendary Rolleiflex, with their 2¼-inch square negatives, and these were superseded in the course of time by 35-mm film cameras offering a big range of interchangeable lenses. Later the cameramen were equipped with Nikon cameras.

Among the photographic staff who made their mark in Humberside were Clarrie

Howson, Jack Davies and Harold ('Tod') Slaughter, who later became Picture Editor. In 1985 the team was headed by Mr Maurice Shepley, assisted by Mr John Paddison.

Communications

The first new agency reports were received on Post Office 'flimsies' – thin, oiled telegraph forms – but after the First World War these began to be replaced by machines developed by Creed for the private conveyance of news between the London news agencies and the provincial newspapers.

When the *Hull Daily Mail* moved to Jameson Street, among the plant transferred was the Creed Wheatstone machine which had been installed in 1922, and which served until an up-to-date multi-channel automatic teleprinter system was introduced in 1948. The Wheatstone machine was operated by Cyril ('Creedo') Daley, who was actually employed by the Press Association and not by the *Hull Daily Mail*. It produced a tape punched with a 'code' of holes, and this was then fed into another machine which transcribed the code into ordinary type at about 100 words a minute, on a single-channel system. 'Creedo' was later joined by Mr Jack Rooms, who served a total of 50 years with the newspaper, latterly as its Chief Telegraphist, and well remembered the coming of the first battery of modern teleprinters in 1948.

Although this voice frequency telegraph system worked at a speed of only 68 words a minute, it operated on six channels simultaneously, giving a total of nearly 400 words a minute. The 1948 system was later replaced by the Creed Envoy eight-channel set, each capable of tapping out 75 words a minute. Tele-typesetting, involving the feeding of news-tapes straight on to a Linotype machine, was possible for quite some time before the change-over to photosetting, but this was never considered a great success. In January, 1985, a new high-speed system, the Newbury 8830 Printer, was installed, giving greater transmission capacity. To give an example, a full, up-to-date race card could be received in under three minutes, compared with 25 minutes under the old system. At peak periods, the new system proved to be 50 minutes ahead of the old, being capable of working at a speed of 1,200 words a minute.

★　★　★　★

The first wired picture published in the *Hull Daily Mail* appeared on September 13, 1941, and illustrated a dramatic story – the surrender of a German submarine to an aircraft piloted by Squadron Leader J. H. Thompson, of Welton, later a well-known Hull businessman. But it was not until 1949 that the *Hull Daily Mail* brought in its own Muirhead telephoto apparatus, complete with portable transmitter which could be used anywhere in the world. The apparatus worked on a simple principle. Two drums, one on the transmitter carrying the picture and one on the receiver bearing sensitised photographic paper, were rotated and traversed, accurately synchronised, by optic heads, which acted as 'magic eyes', transferring the image from the picture to the blank bromide paper. The whole transmission took less than 15 minutes from the beginning of the 'broadcast' to the finished print, while the portable transmitter enabled a cameraman to go to the scene of an event, produce a print on the spot and transmit it to the office.

Later the Muirhead itself gave place to the new Hell Laserstrahl automatic telephoto system, which could pick up the 'white' signal, followed by the phasing signal, to start the transmission of the picture without manual operation. This apparatus was also quicker in the development process because it used a dry silver paper which developed with heat. This paper was installed in the machine itself, and when the picture had finished its traverse after going across the heated roller, it dropped into the basket, ready to be delivered to the photographic section.

Chief Operator was Mr D. Ramsden, assisted by Mr G. C. Coates and Mr D. K. Smith.

The Computer Revolution

For almost 100 years, the Linotype, patented in 1885, and introduced to the *Hull Daily Mail* some 12 years later, had formed the basis of the 'the hot metal system' which remained virtually unchanged all that time. By the 1970's, however, it had become clear that a change to new photoset technology could no longer be delayed. This change was made with some reluctance, for the hot metal system was in some ways more efficient for evening newspaper work, the contents of the pages being more easily changed to up-date each successive edition throughout the afternoon. The old plant and machinery had had its day, however. Spare parts were becoming more and more difficult to obtain as the machines were phased out; and the new system was less labour-intensive – a big consideration in the face of rising wage costs.

Fortunately, however, it was possible to link the new typesetting and plating systems to those grand old work-horses, the Hoe and Crabtree presses, which had continued to play their thunderous music in West Street and South Street since the 1930's. The first major change in the *Hull Daily Mail's* composing room came in 1968, when a number of Linotype operators were re-trained to use a typewriter keyboard, which is considerably different from the large Linotype keyboard.

These operators used a typewriter-like keyboard to punch paper tape with a combination of perforations defining different characters, and this tape of words and spaces was used to drive the Linotype machines, which had a device added to their keyboards to enable them to 'read' the tape. The machines could then run faster than when used manually.

Called 'TTS', this method of composition enabled the newspaper to receive wire-service copy directly on paper tape for later use on the Linotypes. Race cards, stocks and shares and the General Election results were transmitted from Manchester to Hull, where the signals were received and converted into punched paper tape.

★   ★   ★   ★

The *Hull Daily Mail's* first computer, the Muirhead Muset, was installed in 1969. This allowed the operators on the Fairchild and AKI TTS keyboards to set words and spaces, leaving the computer, which had the widths of each character of type in its memory, to calculate and 'justify' each line of type, to make it fill the line.

The application of computers was to lead to a complete break with the hot metal machines in the years to come. In 1974, the newspaper purchased one of the first mini-computers, the Dec PDP8/e, with a typesetting programme to drive the typesetters without spacebands. This was done by having five fixed spaces, a combination of which was used for each word space, and when a line was complete, it was 'quaded' centre, thus giving an appearance of being justified.

Photo-typesetting came in 1977, with the introduction of the Photon Pacesetter Mk. III and IV, which had 16 typefaces in a full range with a speed of 150 newspaper lines per minute. Varisystem 3216 keyboards were used to punch the paper tape to be used on the Photons, and the output from the Photons was a photographic image in positive form, which was subsequently pasted up for making into a printing plate.

Starting first with display advertising, the next step in the demise of the Linotype came in 1978 with the installation of the Comprite Newspaper System, and this meant that all operators now had to be re-trained to use the typewriter keyboard. The Comprite system served the *Hull Daily Mail* well, allowing all the editorial matter and classified advertisements to be set in this way. When a classified advertisement was 'input' and stored on the 12-million character disc storage system, it was coded so that the system would 'output' the advertisement on the nights it was due to appear. The system also enabled the Advertisement Department to have an accurate lineage report of the amount of classified advertising, to aid page planning.

* * * *

Although there was still one Linecaster left, which was used for the Stop Press, the last hot metal page to leave the 'stone' – the bench on which the pages used to be made up – was in 1978; since then, the whole of the paper has been set by computerised techniques.

The Photon Pacesetters were replaced in 1980 by more up-to-date digitised typesetting, where the bromide paper is exposed to a light-source from a CRT tube, each character being made up of a series of scan-lines on the tube.

The Comprite system, which used one of the original Dec computers purchased for TTS, was replaced in the spring of 1984 by the most sophisticated system in provincial newspapers – the Atex Newspaper System, which boasted twin 80-mb disk drives 765k memory in each of two CPU's. Twenty keyboards were also on line to the computers; three Lineprinters and two Linotype 202 Photo-typesetters were also on line.

This saw the end of paper tape; each operator had his own VDT screen to view the file on which he was working.

The system handled unlimited classified headings and any schedule of run days possible. It also generated advertising reports for lineage and re-solicitation reports for advertisements which were about to finish their scheduled run in any of our publications.

* * * *

In 1985 the Composing Room Manager was Mr K. D. Green, his deputy, Mr Peter J. Martin, and Mr S. Potts Assistant Manager. Mr G. C. Burton was Platemaking Manager and his deputy Mr A. G. Harding. And Mr C. Windass was Manager of the Machine Department, assisted by Mr S. Smith.

The Years of Change

No sooner had the *Hull Daily Mail* settled into 84-86 Jameson Street than the winds of change began blowing a positive gale through its Delft-dadoed corridors. The next four years were to see momentous events flashing by with unbelievable rapidity, bringing both expansion and changes of ownership.

In 1927, the Grotrian brothers and their co-directors bought another family newspaper, the *Grimsby Evening Telegraph*, which had belonged to the Doughty's. And in July, 1928, they sold a half-interest in the whole business to a new combine which was in process of being formed under the title of Provincial Newspapers.

The 'parents' of Provincial were United Newspapers and the giant Inveresk Paper Company. In 1918, a group of men associated with the wartime Prime Minister, David Lloyd George, had bought two highly reputable newspapers, the *Daily Chronicle* and *Lloyds' Sunday News*, from the Lloyd family at a cost of £1,600,000, forming a new company called United Newspapers Ltd.

They added a number of provincial publications and then, in 1926, sold out to a group headed by the Marquis of Reading. The sum paid, in cash and shares, was £2,900,000; and there was a clause written into the agreement that the papers 'should be conducted in accordance with the policy of Progressive Liberalism, in opposition on the one hand to reactionary doctrines and on the other hand to communistic or revolutionary doctrines, and that consistent support shall be given to the promotion of unity in the Liberal Party and to the furtherance of social and industrial reform through the Land Policy, Coal and Power Policy, Industrial Policy, Free Trade, etc, and other programmes of Liberal and Radical measures adopted by the Liberal Party'.

Lloyd George, who had been named in the agreement as the 'sole vendor', came in for much criticism for appearing to have his cake, in the form of continuing political backing, and eat it to the tune of an estimated £1-million profit. Lord Reading's chairmanship was of short duration; just a year later, he sold out to William Harrison, a self-made Yorkshire lawyer of whom Guy Schofield, in his history of United Newspapers, *The Men that Carry the News*, wrote, 'Nobody so completely justifies the cliché, "a meteoric career". He came, he flared, he went out. And when he was quenched, men stared for a space at the cinders.'

By the mid-1920's, Harrison had become chairman of the Inveresk Paper Company, and, in 1926, he acquired the *Illustrated London News*, the *Sphere*, the *Tatler*, the *Bystander* and other periodicals, which he combined as Illustrated Newspapers Ltd. Then, ranging the provinces, he added to his 'bag' the *Lancashire Daily Post* and *Preston Guardian*, together with the *Northampton Chronicle*. In July, 1928, he purchased the Daily Chronicle Investment Company (United Newspapers) and the deal with the Hull newspapers went through at about the same time, creating, with the addition of a number of other titles in Scotland and the North of England, owned or part-owned, the firm of Provincial Newspapers Ltd.

Edgar Grotrian, H. Brent Grotrian and Lt. Col. James Walker, another Hull director, known to the staff as 'Jimmy the One', joined the Provincial board, along with such distinguished figures as Mr B. H. Binder (later Sir Bernhard Binder), Sir Harry Brittain, Jack Akerman, former assistant manager of *The Times* and R. W. Crabtree, of the Leeds firm of printing machinery manfacturers.

Little more than a year later, the Harrison 'empire' began to crumble. William Harrison had over-reached himself and the Inveresk company was in deep financial trouble, while United Newspapers were also heavily in debt.

Harrison's brief career as a newspaper tycoon had ended. Directors Binder, Akerman and Herbert Brent Grotrian pulled the chestnuts out of the fire – but only at the cost of sacrificing the excellent *Daily Chronicle*, which was merged with the *Daily News* and virtually lost its identity.

Local mergers – and a pledge
Meanwhile, the *Hull Daily Mail's* rivals, the *Eastern Morning News* group, had been getting deeper and deeper into the financial mire, too. Their troubles had started as far back as 1922. The *Evening News* became involved in a Crown prosecution for conducting a lottery. Then, the paper made the mistake of copying the *Hull Daily Mail's* popular 'Final City' seal. The *Mail* took legal action and substantial damages were awarded to the company. The *News* group could not meet the heavy litigation costs, whereupon the *Hull Daily Mail* paid the bill, and, under a private agreement, took a lien on the *Hull Evening News*.

The group continued its precarious existence under its own steam until 1929-30, when it finally collapsed, and the *Hull Daily Mail* took over those members of its editorial and works staff whom it could absorb. The first casualty was the *Eastern Morning News*, which, on November 8, 1929, was merged with the *Evening News*. The following day, the weekly *Hull News* was incorporated into the same medium. The paper struggled hopelessly for five more months, but could not make ends meet and was amalgamated into the *Hull Daily Mail*.

Like a condemned man smiling bravely on the way to the scaffold, the *Evening News* carried a buoyant and cheerful last editorial on April 17, 1930:

'The *Evening News* and the *Daily Mail* have been friendly rivals for many years,' it said. 'They will now join forces, and, as the improvements planned are carried out, will provide Hull and district with an evening journal second to none in the country.

'The case for amalgamation is unanswerable. Newspaper production has become far more costly and complex. Great circulation is the essential condition on which readers and advertisers can be given the best service. Combination and concentration will benefit both.

'The new *Daily Mail* will continue all the best features of the existing papers, will add to them, and in these ways enhance its popularity and usefulness.

'The new *Daily Mail* will be a still more representative and powerful voice of the great industries and institutions on which the prosperity and welfare of Hull depend. Great as the city is today, its future will be greater far. *The Daily Mail* will co-operate with all who are striving to exalt its place in the world.'

Being the only daily paper in the city, the editorial explained, the new *Daily Mail* would recognise a special responsibility to be strictly fair and impartial in its reporting of local affairs.

'No sectional interest will have preferential treatment in the news columns. In municipal as well as in national politics, all parties will have opportunity to present their case to the public, with whom rests the final judgment.'

It was in this editorial that the pledge of party political independence was made to the people of Hull:

'The *Daily Mail* has taken a leading part in the political life of Hull for nearly half a century. It has seen many changes. There used to be only two parties. Now there are three. It is the continual debate between them which decides questions of the most intimate concern to the whole people.

'The newspaper's duty is to supply its readers with an impartial record of the views of all parties. The *Daily Mail* will be an Independent organ of opinion. Its own views will be expressed frankly and fearlessly in the editorial columns. But these views will never be allowed to influence its larger duty of providing a newspaper in which all interests shall be sure of fair treatment. "The Truth in the News" will be a guiding maxim for the *Daily Mail*. While no human foresight and care can eliminate all error, the utmost vigilance will be exercised, and readers may be certain that the news in the *Daily Mail* is honest and free of intentional taint or twist.'

Equally prophetic and far-sighted was the newspaper's promise of sex-equality: 'Newspapers used to be written for men only. When "Women's Features" were introduced they were merely side shows; it was not realised that in most of the important things of life men's interests are also women's interests, and that the ideal newspaper should cater equally for both. All that is now changed. More than ever before, the *Daily Mail* will supply the needs of wives and daughters as well as of husbands and sons.

'A faithful record of events in an imperfect world must necessarily include much that is disagreeable and painful. As hitherto, the truth about things good and bad will be told in the *Daily Mail* with restraint. In every way the paper will continue to be a paper for the home – fit for the home, keeping the home in touch every day with the pulsing life of the city, of the nation, and of the world.

'The responsibility of newspaper service is very great. The *Daily Mail* will try to be worthy of it, and so to justify the fullest confidence of its readers.'

SELDOM CAN THE AIMS AND OBJECTS OF A RESPONSIBLE
PROVINCIAL NEWSPAPER HAVE BEEN BETTER EXPRESSED.

The Ace in the Pack

In 1930, another threat arose to the existing provincial papers. In the words of Guy Schofield: 'A newspaper Nero was flaunting his purple. Lord Rothermere, at the head at the great *Daily Mail* organisation, had launched his grandiose scheme for a chain of new papers – *Evening Worlds* – in various big centres of population.' High on the list of those centres was Hull, together with Cardiff, Middlesbrough, Sheffield and Birmingham, and plans were under consideration covering Edinburgh, Preston, Liverpool, Leeds and Belfast. *Evening Worlds* were already established in Newcastle and Bristol, though the former was quickly ousted by the home-grown *Newcastle Chronicle*.

Somewhat arrogantly, it was thought, Lord Rothermere indicated that these new evening newspapers would bring slick, London-type journalism to the provinces in place of the homely, parish-pump 'local rag' to which the people were accustomed.

But His Lordship, whose personality, Guy Schofield stresses, was in remarkable contrast to that of his 'sagacious and modest successor', the second Lord Rothermere, had reckoned without local pride and taste.

Despite the Newcastle fiasco, however, he pressed on with the idea of establishing an *Evening World* in Hull, and a huge notice-board was erected in Carr Lane, near the old Grosvenor Hotel, announcing that this was the chosen site. 'Whether it was serious, or whether it was just window-dressing to force a takeover of the *Hull Daily Mail*, I do not know,' says R. A. Brewer in his *History of Hull Newspapers*.

As Herbert Brent Grotrian knew, the Hull readers were unlikely to transfer their allegiance to such an upstart, but, with Provincial Newspapers in such a parlous state at that period, this was no time to put it to the test, especially as there were other, less well-established publications to consider.

So Provincial and the Hull directors decided to 'play their ace' – the *Hull Daily Mail* and *Times*. 'An adroit compromise was effected, the indefatigable Bernhard Binder acting as Provincial's negotiator,' records Guy Schofield. 'On condition that he kept out of all other territories where Provincial Newspapers functioned, Lord Rothermere was sold the controlling interest in the *Hull Daily Mail* and its associated publications. Provincial retained a 49 per cent interest, and that 49 per cent was to play an important part in the successful expansion of the group many years later.'

★　★　★　★

Despite the fact that the *Hull Daily Mail* had been used as bait, in a manner of speaking, to buy off the threat to the whole Provincial Newspapers structure, the move did not damage its editorial autonomy or dilute its local flavour. Lord Rothermere soon abandoned his idea of pressing smart, quasi-nationals on an unwilling provincial readership, and his Northcliffe Newspapers Group, named after his famous brother, was built on the process of acquiring existing properties and allowing them to carry on very much as before.

Edgar Grotrian was to go on sitting in his fumed oak office in Jameson Street until June, 1937, when he retired. He is remembered by the staff of that era as a somewhat hard man, unlike his liberal-minded father, and one who listened with less than sympathy to claims for wage-increases, however well justified. But it must be remembered that under his management the company flourished, the prodigious task of building the new offices and transferring to them plant and personnel was accomplished, and the wheeling and dealing in the company's shares had been negotiated without the readership knowing much about it.

And, when one contemplates the happenings of a year such as 1930, when, with Provincial Newspapers hovering on the edge of bankruptcy, the *Hull Daily Mail* took over the opposition papers, concluded the Rothermere deal, modernised the layout of the paper while still reeling from the suicide of the editor – and still produced those superb Amy Johnson 'specials' – the verdict must surely be 'Not bad – not bad at all!'

Edgar Grotrian was also human enough to enjoy a day at the races, and he functioned as a successful tipster in the sports pages under the pseudon of 'Gee-Gee'. He also played an important role in the establishment of the Rediffusion wired radio service in Hull.

Sir Herbert Brent Grotrian, who was MP for South West Hull in the 1920's, was to have a distinguished career with Provincial Newspapers, holding the chairmanship from 1930 to 1947, when he handed over to Harley Drayton. Sir Herbert's son, Mr J. A. D. Grotrian (later Sir John Grotrian), joined the Provincial board in 1948, continuing the family tradition of involvement in the newspaper industry, even though the Hull connection was finally to be severed.

It was, incidentally, in 1930 that the limited company of Hull and Grimsby Newspapers was formed.

A New Look

The *Hull Daily Mail* may have been saved from the threat of losing its identity under a coat of gaudy Fleet Street paint, but that is not to say that it could not, at that stage, do with a bit of brightening up. It was in 1930 that news appeared on the front page for the first time in place of small advertisements – a change heralded in the valedictory *Evening News* editorial previously quoted.

The task was given to a young sub-editor who had joined the staff seven years before – Arthur Brewer. 'Well, of course, that was egg and milk to me – a young man aged about 30; so I – prophetically as it turned out – based my style on that of the London *Daily Mail* layout, and, with what type we had, made 'splash' headlines on the front page and inside,' he recalled. Mr Brewer later received the MBE for his services to journalism.

The transformation was carried out under a considerable emotional cloud, however, for the shy but likeable Edgar Wills Lewis had recently taken his own life. He was having domestic trouble at the time, and it was generally believed that this was the main reason for the tragedy; but Mr Brewer recalls that when Provincial Newspapers acquired their interest in the business, they introduced their own editor, Mr W. S. Robinson.

'For a few weeks there was a very strained situation for everybody, because the two editors, Lewis and Robinson, walked around together, and nobody at first knew who was the "Big Chief". There were divided loyalties and Lewis gave it out that he could have modernised the paper had he been given the chance.' At all events, Mr Lewis gassed himself at his Hornsea home shortly afterwards. 'Mr Robinson went away for a few days, leaving the Assistant Editor Mr J. B. Chapman, in charge,' says Mr Brewer.

W. S. Robinson, or 'Robbie', as he was known, came from Leeds and had substantial experience in both national and provincial journalism. He was an immensely popular man, and it was he who was to guide the editorial fortunes of the paper for the next 16 years, which included the dark days of the Second World War. 'He was a perfect gentleman', says Mr Brewer. 'He got his own way, but always in a nice, gentlemanly manner.'

★　★　★　★

In 1933, the directors were confronted once more with the necessity to expand mechanical capacity to meet the enormously increased demands of a considerably larger circulation.

They took what the chairman of the time, Mr W. A. McWhirter, described as 'the courageous step' of installing new machinery at a cost of more than £80,000 – a prodigious sum in those days – to give Hull one of the most modern newspaper works in the country. Mr McWhirter, incidentally, was the father of the celebrated McWhirter twin brothers, compilers of the *Guinness Book of Records*. With customary pomp and civic participation, the new machinery was set in motion by the Lord Mayor of the day, Alderman Arthur Shepherd.

The Stories We Could Not Tell

From that point up to the outbreak of war, the record was one of continued progress and growing influence.

On Edgar Grotrian's retirement in 1937, his place was taken by the popular and charming H. V. ('Sam') Weller. Mr Weller, who had made rapid progress in the Northcliffe Group, being appointed a general manager at the age of 25, came to Hull from the *Staffordshire Evening Sentinel*.

The Jameson Street buildings came out of the 1939-45 conflict relatively unscathed, being one of the few large concerns in the city to escape major damage or total destruction. Those escapes were on many occasions narrow enough to be almost miraculous, and throughout the war publication remained unbroken. The newspaper's problems – severely restricted supplies, destruction of paper cargoes at sea or in depots ashore, acute staff shortages, interrupted communications, censorship and rail isolation, to mention a few – were in all conscience harassing enough, but were relatively light compared with those of firms whose property and plant were razed to the ground.

During the major Blitzes of May, 1941, the *Hull Daily Mail* office stood relatively undamaged in a sea of fire and devastation. A member of the staff making for the office at 5 am after one of the raids, asked a police officer on the perimeter of the destruction how the *Hull Daily Mail* office had fared. He was told, 'It has gone up in smoke.' But he made his way through to find that, apart from hundreds of broken windows and a few cracked walls, the office had escaped. Hammond's department store nearby was wrecked and in flames. Fire had spread to W. H. Smith and Sons across the road; and Jameson Street was in a sorry state. On another occasion, a landmine which blasted the Metropole Dance Hall, the Builders' Exchange, a number of shops and two public houses in West Street spared the *Hull Daily Mail* office major damage.

★ ★ ★ ★

The staff worked amid broken glass, the fine North lights of the Composing Room were blacked out by boards, and not the least of the difficulties was caused by the splinters of glass which had showered on to cases of type.

Mention of that 5 am start prompts a member of staff to recall the long hours worked in those days:

'Before the war, we had persisted with a 7 o'clock edition, which, so far as I could see, was useless, because by then the radio was in most homes and they had the 7 o'clock news summary, which was later than anything we could do, because our so-called 7 o'clock edition was only a stop-press cricket score affair,' recalls R. A. Brewer. 'However, with the wartime air raids starting at tea-time in the winter, the newsboys refused to deliver after dark, so the last edition went to press about 5 o'clock and we were able to go home at tea-time, and generally before dark, for which we were very thankful.'

This left the *Hull Daily Mail* with five editions, starting at about 1 pm with the City Issue and following this with Late City, Final City, Last Issue and Extra editions. This system persisted until the advent of the photoset method of production, since when four editions, designated one, two, three and four star, have been produced.

During the war, Editor 'Robbie' did not shrink from taking his turn on firewatching duties, and other members of the editorial staff who shared the dangers and discomforts, along with works and commercial personnel, included John Gosse, who was later called up for military service, and who sent back, as one of the first members of the Allied Forces into Belsen Concentration Camp, the grimmest story the newspaper has ever told. Chief Reporter Don Giles, Chief Photographer Clarrie Howson, Ernest ('Tim') Underwood, for many years the paper's fishing correspondent (later awarded the M.B.E.) and Vic Moorhouse were also there.

When the telegraphic system failed on the morning after one Blitz, Mr Moorhouse made a dash to Leeds to collect from another Northcliffe office, the *Evening News*, all available 'set' copy. He returned to the still-smoking city to find that the copy was not needed, however, as skilled and efficient work had got the lines functioning again. Vic Moorhouse also remembers nights spent at the theatre with the strains of 'The Flowers that Bloom in the Spring' contrasting with the 'crump' of the ak-ak fire outside, and recalls how he and other firewatchers shared a warming bottle of rum with theatrical entrepreneur Harold Clarke on the night the Tivoli variety theatre caught fire.

And it was 'Moorhouse of the Mail', as he came to be known, who covered the wartime visits of King George VI and Queen Elizabeth to the bomb-shattered city, and followed Prime Minister Winston Churchill round on his tour of the stricken areas. Vic was present at the historic gathering in the Guildhall, commemorated in a painting which now hangs in the Banqueting Hall there, and he also recalls that as Churchill was touring the docks, the inevitable cigar between his teeth, a docker shouted, 'Chuck us the butt!' 'Winnie' did.

As Churchill was leaving, Vic Moorhouse pressed him for a parting message for the people of Hull. Gruffly, the great man grunted a few words. Vic quickly phrased them into a more articulate form and asked, 'Would that be all right, Mr Churchill?' The Prime Minister nodded approval, grunted again, and was on his way. The copy had to be sent to London for censorship, and for security reasons the story of Churchill's visit could not be released until he had left the city.

★   ★   ★   ★

Many of the best stories of that time could not be told – the building of part of the Mulberry Harbour on the Humber Bank, numerous sea disasters, and, most bizarre of all, perhaps, the secret conveyance through Hull of a vast quantity of Dutch silver bullion, en route for America via Liverpool. The bullion was loaded on to a train, guarded only by a police sergeant armed with a 1914 revolver, and it was held up for hours by a mechanical breakdown at Blacktoft, but eventually the precious freight got through.

Much of the *Daily Mail's* own vital equipment was dispersed in the countryside as a safeguard against damage to the office. This included a number of Linotype

The height of the blaze at the Cleveland Street mill.

Wartime firemen: battered, bleeding – but still smiling.

machines which were stored as far as 50 miles away, and were regularly serviced for use. Hundreds of tons of newsprint were similarly scattered, and daily journeys were made to bring in supplies for current editions. Delivery vans and priceless files of earlier newspapers also figured in Operation Dispersal. Ironically, while goods and machinery were being taken to safety a number of people from the surrounding area were sleeping in the *Hull Daily Mail's* basement, which was also used as an air raid shelter by staff during daytime alerts.

Mrs C. M. Green, who, as Cicely Spurr, worked as secretary to the Accountant, Mr Leslie Call, also has graphic memories of the war years:

'I remember the 1941 raids, and the morning after, when it was some time before I was allowed along West Street to get into work,' she later wrote. 'When I was able to enter the building, I found the floors covered in glass several inches deep. The Accounts department was evacuated to the Board Room, where I was given a small, flimsy table to work on. It was just big enough for my typewriter and notebook, which was balanced on the edge. When I returned the typewriter carriage, the table skidded several inches along the polished floor, which rather upset the rhythm until I worked out another rhythm of returning the carriage with one hand and holding the table with the other. After some time the glass was replaced and we returned to the ground floor for one day, but that night the bombers came again, and once more the floors had disappeared under broken glass, so it was back to the Board Room until the windows were boarded up – no glass this time.'

Mrs Green also remembers how on one occasion during those days of four-page papers, she 'nearly gave Mr Weller a heart attack' by making a typing error indicating that the paper had used 20 lb of newsprint above the allocation. This brought a stiff letter from the Ministry of Supply, informing the General Manager that the *Hull Daily Mail's* Return of Newsprint Used showed that the regulations had not been complied with, and going on to remind him of the penalties for such misdemeanour, including confiscation of all newsprint stocks, which could not be replaced. 'Sammy's doing his nut,' Leslie Call reported to his secretary, who traced the error, wrote a letter of explanation and took it to Mr Weller to sign. 'When I went into his office he had a very worried look, which was relieved somewhat when he read the letter. He signed it and we heard no more. I sometimes think of that 20 lb of' newsprint when I see the amount of paper used these days.'

★　★　★　★

Mrs Green also remembers the time when a Linotype operator threatened to report her to the Father of the Chapel (Shop steward): 'This arose because the firewatchers had to sign a book which was placed near the West Street door. This book had to be available for inspection by the authorities and from it I passed on the names to the cashier, who would pay 10s to each man for each firewatching duty. Occasionally, someone forgot to sign, and one man always 'forgot', and always objected very strongly when I went to see him the next morning for his signature.

'After several such incidents, I told Mr Call and he said, 'Well, don't pay him.' The next time the signature was missing, I left the name off the list to the cashier, so the man came to see me, in quite a temper. 'He was in more of a temper when he left, because I very politely, tongue in cheek, pointed out to him that his name was not in the book and my instructions were to pass on to the cashier the names of people who had signed the book. 'Shortly after this, the phone rang and Mr Call

Hammonds store after the blitz of 7 May 1941. The Mail building, further right, not only survived but never missed an issue.

answered it. He went out and said that I was to be reported to the Father of the Chapel. I wasn't – and the next time that man was on firewatching duty, he did sign the book!'

Another part of Cicely's work involved taking special photographic orders. One day she was called to the counter to see an American soldier who wanted a photograph of a shop in Paragon Street selling horsemeat for human consumption. 'He wanted to send a photograph home so that the people in America could see some of the conditions we had to bear. He didn't get his photograph, of course: there were other uses for the photographic supplies.'

No account of the *Hull Daily Mail's* work during the Second World War would be complete without a reference to its Comforts for the Forces Fund, to which readers contributed a magnificent total of £50,000.

The Creed machine showing national news coming through on perforated tape.

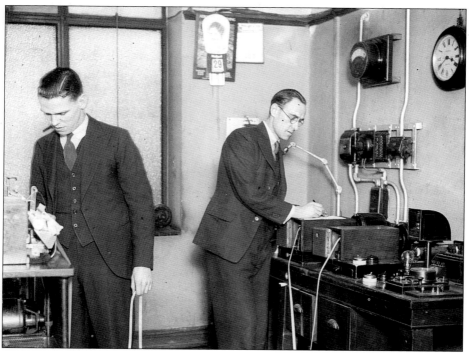

In Ever-Widening Circles

Producing an article is one thing: distributing it is another. And, as with so many other things in our story, the history of the *Hull Daily Mail's* widening circulation area follows the history of advancing technology, this time in the field of transportation. The 'brave, unwearied feet' of the army of news-boys collecting their supplies from the publishing department could carry the news only so far. To get it to readers in the outlying areas required one of Man's earliest inventions – the wheel – powered first by flesh-and-blood horsepower and latterly by that vested in the internal combustion engine.

The first newspaper vans were horse-drawn. The distribution of the papers to shops was in the hands of a private firm, Hancocks, who conveyed them in vans supported on two large wheels. By 1912, the *Hull Daily Mail* had a fleet of four delivery vans 'of the latest type' in two of which the driver sat exposed to the elements while the papers remained snug and dry in the enclosed part behind him; and two three-wheelers affording their drivers some protection by means of an overhead canopy, though the sides of the cab were still open. These vans were augmented by a number of 'Auto carriers', three-wheeled motorcycles with a large box at the front to hold the papers. Mr Arthur Clarkson, the *Hull Daily Mail's* former Transport Manager, recalls that three of those were still in existence until the Second World War, when they were destroyed by a bomb which fell in Lansdowne Street. After the First World War, when equipment was in short supply, the fleet was augmented by a converted ex-Army ambulance.

★　★　★　★

The newspaper's first Transport Department was in Mill Street, on a site formerly occupied by Binns car park, and there it remained until 1922, when it was moved to Lansdowne Street, where the *Eastern Morning News* group also kept its vehicles. So, when the *Hull Daily Mail* moved to Jameson Street, hard by the old Mill Street site, the fleet had already moved on, and was based some way off, though the commemoration booklet of 1926 records that there was 'an emergency call garage in the main building'.

For quite some time, recalls Mr Clarkson, there were no newsagents handling the company's papers beyond the Haworth Arms, on Beverley Road, Wheeler Street, on Anlaby Road, and the Transport Sheds on Holderness Road. Country parcels went by train, while carriers conveyed the weekly newspapers out to the villages along with the other supplies they picked up in the city. Only with the development of rural bus services were many of the villagers able to get the evening *Mail* delivered regularly.

As a point of interest for industrial historians, Works Manager Harry Brown, who was in charge of the old *Hull Daily Mail* garage in Mill Street, later started the City Engraving Company.

'As the news-agencies sprang up further and further away, we put on our own transport, until we were taking in Willerby, Anlaby, Kirkella and Westella, eventually moving out as far as Goole,' recalled Mr Clarkson. A branch was opened in Market Weighton, followed by one in Bridington, and, in the fulness of time, others were set up in Beverley, Driffield, Scarborough, Goole and Brigg, and editorial bases established in Hornsea, Withernsea and in Barton-on-Humber.

For important events such as royal weddings, coronations and the like, elaborate arrangements were often made involving planes and fast dispatch-riders to bring the precious photographic plates to the office in time to catch the edition. And on days when Hull City FC played Grimsby, a motor launch brought the plates to the quayside on the North Bank, where they were picked up by a motorcyclist who sped them back to catch the *Sports Mail*. 'During the last war, when the river was mined or there was an air-raid warning in progress, we had a motor-boat standing by to take our edition across to New Holland Pier when the ferry-boats were not running,' said Mr Clarkson, who himself used to drive to Barnetby to put papers on the train for the Grimsby and Scunthorpe area. 'I used to give the guard 6d to see that the papers reached their destination, and recouped it from the cashier the following Friday.'

The un-bridged Humber was in those days a formidable barrier, as it had been for centuries. On one occasion, a van sped from Brigg Office to New Holland hoping to catch the ferry with an important parcel. The driver arrived as the ferry was pulling away from the jetty. A member of the crew, trying to be helpful, shouted, 'Chuck it, Charlie!' Charlie chucked it – and missed. The contents are still at the bottom of the Humber.

⋆ ⋆ ⋆ ⋆

But if things were difficult for the Transport Department during the war, worse was to follow. The Lansdowne Street property had received a direct hit, and 300 tons of newsprint stored there were lost. The building was repaired, but when the adjacent Western General Hospital was developed into the great new Hull Royal Infirmary in the 1960's, the garage site was needed for inclusion in the scheme as part of the School of Nursing.

Long years before, plans had been made for the building of a new garage, but it was difficult to obtain Town Planning permission for such an amenity close to the city centre, for obvious reasons, and a search had to be made for off-centre accommodation. For months, General Manager John T. Paterson and Arthur Clarkson scoured the town, rejecting property after unsuitable property, until they came upon a collection of old buildings and a piece of land in St James Street, off Hessle Road, and this was finally developed into the newspaper's present Transport Department, housing its up-to-date fleet of vans and cars. One of Arthur Clarkson's memories is that among the 'assets' taken over with the property was an ancient donkey-engine, still in working order. The search ended just in time, for work had already begun on the Infirmary scheme, and this virtually put the *Hull Daily Mail* garage 'out on the street', a massive drainage system being dug right through Lansdowne Street.

In 1984 Mr Brian Levine oversaw a fleet of nearly 70 vehicles; but the saga of how, over the years, the *Hull Daily Mail* and *Times* van drivers have kept the deliveries flowing through all kinds of weather conditions – rain, hail, tempest and deep snowdrifts on the Wolds – not to mention the hazards of war, could in itself furnish material for a book, and merits sincere tribute here.

Promoting the Product

If speedy and efficient transporation is vital to a group of newspapers, it is equally important to ensure that the right edition, carrying the right contents, gets to the right readership at the right place in the right quantities at the right time. The exacting task belongs to the Circulation Department.

Yet, strangely enough, in the early days newspapers had no circulation departments as such. The job was shared between the Publishing and Transport Departments. Representatives were, however, employed, selling advertisement space, promoting circulation or carrying out commercial duties such as debt--collecting. There were also a number of Special Commissioners on the staff, including Mr E. E. Lewis, to whom reference has already been made and they were 'sent across the seas upon important missions to Continental and Dominion cities and ports with which Hull has commercial relations'.

In their efforts to gain sales, some newspapers offered incentives, such as cheap insurance, to their customers. The job of the Circulation Department is to find out what the public wants from its local newspaper and report back to the managerial and editorial departments so that they can, as far as possible, fulfil those wants. The department then oversees the distribution of the various editions accordingly, throughout a 1,001-square-mile area.

Research teams were constantly at work throughout the area, interviewing newsagents and their customers and asking for their views, while, back at the main office, Circulation Manager Richard Dodd, working with colleagues in the other departments, ironed out any difficulties concerning transport, the timing of 'runs' and similar matters.

The department was, in short, charged with the task of promoting the product. It has always been responsible for the attractive and useful stands which appear at agricultural shows and other public events, the award-winning floats in the Lord Mayor's annual parade, and, more recently, television advertising, bingo promotions and competitions. Possibly no other department has changed more radically in recent years. At one time, newsagents took their supplies on an easy sale-or-return basis. Today, this is a hard-sell industry, with no quarter asked or given. While in previous years advertising accounted for by far the largest share of the newspaper's revenue, circulation is now catching up, and in 1984, 31.19 per cent of the company's revenue came from the sale of newspapers. To maintain, and, if possible, increase this figure requires keen business methods, and the department's work involves constantly seeking new outlets and closing down unprofitable ones.

* * * *

Being the shrewd businessmen they were, the founders of the *Hull Daily Mail* must have realised that, even at 1885 prices, the costs of starting a new publication from scratch, with new premises, plant and staff, would be prohibitive. That was why they were content to begin in a small way, taking over the antiquated equipment of the *Packet* and building up from there.

The number of copies printed daily on the old flatbed press must have been minute by today's reckoning. But the success of the new venture soon began to tell, and, with the rapid acquisition of new plant and machinery, the circulation figures began to rise . . . . and rise.

The 1912 brochure proudly records that 'the number of copies of the *Hull Daily Mail* sold during the 1912 period was over 200,000 in excess of the number sold during the 1911 period'. In 1921, the published circulation figure was 60,578 a day; and by 1925 when the new Jameson Street building was going up, it had risen to 65,134. By 1934, the presses were pounding out 80,000 copies a day, in 1938 the figure had grown to 83,000, and it continued to rise until World War II brought restrictions and shortages in all consumer goods.

But the boom time for the Hull newspaper was to come in the postwar years. Full employment and the 'affluent society' meant that everyone could afford a newspaper. The replacement of the little terraces, where one copy would be passed round every home during the evening, by the new housing estates where neighbours were not so intimate, meant that more copies were being sold. The paper was the only source of local news, and, in the course of an afternoon, one person might buy several editions to gain up-to-the-minute information about racing or cricket results, or some other matter in which he or she was particularly interested.

In 1973, the circulation was 135,000 a day, and in 1974, it peaked at 137,000. The *Sports Mail* enjoyed spectacular success during those years, while the *Times* Series, covering the rural areas of East Yorkshire and North Lincolnshire proved popular with the farming and country folk, and the *Hull Times*, refurbished in the 1950's as a bright, magazine-type weekly recording the city scene, enjoyed a circulation bonanza during the meteoric rise to fame of popular Hull ballad singer David Whitfield, whose life-story it ran as a series.

The *Times* Series actually pre-dated Hull and Grimsby Newspapers, which finally absorbed them. The earliest was the *Hull Times*, which curiously enough circulated on the South Bank, being started in 1856. It later became the *Hull and Linconshire Times* and later just the *Lincolnshire Times*, evolving into the *Lincolnshire and South Humberside Times* in 1974. *The Hull and Yorkshire Times* commenced publication in 1867 and continued until 1984.

The recession of the 1970's, together with the proliferation of other media – BBC and commercial local radio, TV and the various data services – were bound to have their effect on local newspapers, but, through the introduction of bright new features and the maintenance of its superb advertising services, the *Hull Daily Mail* has managed to hold its own, the published figures for 1984 being 113,945 and 1985, 110,730 copies per day.

★   ★   ★   ★

Following a trend, the company introduced its popular free newspaper, the *Hull Star*, in 1980, and this was followed in May, 1984, by the *Bridlington Star*. These freely-distributed journals tended to replace the weeklies, and in 1984 the North Bank editions of the *Times* Series ceased publication, leaving only the *Lincolnshire and South Humberside Times*. The Circulation Department was now fully computerised. At the time of writing in 1984 Mr P. F. H. Lonsdale was Circulation Field Sales Manager, Mr Frank Milner, the Publisher, and his assistant Mr E. Perrin.

The Sports Desk in Jameson Street, 1984, still using typewriters but with television, a sign of the technological changes which were gathering pace.

Vital Role of Advertising

It is, of course, a part of media history that the development of advertising was the greatest single factor in freeing newspapers from dependence on Party political funds. By diversifying their sources of revenue in this way, newspapers were able to maintain a steady income, and this enabled their editorial voices to speak ever more freely, in the knowledge that, whatever vested interests they found it necessary to challenge, no one institution or individual, however powerful, could exert a financial stranglehold over them. The *Hull Daily Mail* and its associated publications were no exception, and, as its advertising services developed from small beginnings – quaint and crude, perhaps, by today's sophisticated standards – they gradually evolved into a unique shop-window for the trader and a superb service to the customer.

Mention has already been made of the Births, Marriages and Deaths column, which Professor Richard Hoggart found such a rich source of latter-day folk custom for his best-selling survey of the 1950's, *The Uses of Literacy*. The 'small ads' have always served as a particularly personal link between the *Mail* and its readers, recording the most intimate landmarks of their lives, reuniting friends and relatives through personal announcements, and ranging from the mundane business of buying and selling second-hand goods to the recovery of dearly-loved pets and lost treasures – the free 'Found' section is much appreciated – or putting employer and work-seeker in touch with one another to their mutual profit. The Local Authority also makes extensive use of the advertisement columns for the publication of notices – in fact, the obligation that Statutory and legal notices must be so published within the area concerned would appear, in itself, to guarantee a future for local newspapers!

Recent years have seen the extension of the composite advertisement feature, and fine examples are to be seen on the newspaper's files. Artists and feature editors combine with advertisement department staff to provide an excellent service to advertiser and reader. Today, the Advertisement Department is one of the most technically advanced in the whole organisation, fully computerised and including the highly-successful 'Housefinder' service as part of its property services.

The *Hull Daily Mail* is a firm supporter of the principles laid down within the British Code of Advertising Practice in matters of care, truth and integrity in copy and presentation. It is from this department, too, that many reader services and much reader involvement are planned under the direction of the Advertising Features Manager. These include the popular cruises, spring and autumn fashion shows, exhibitions and competitions.

Older readers will recall with affection some of the personalities who have headed the department over the years, including the genial Joe Hallowell, who hailed from Newcastle, and whose extra-mural activities included writing children's stories and arranging charity shows.

Joe, as everyone knew him, was succeeded by Colonel George Macdonald, who was made an MBE for his wartime services on Montgomery's planning staff, and who has since made his mark as a tireless worker for the Sailors' Children's Society and Merchant Navy Hotel. Then came Mr Robert (Bob) Crawley, who also did much to build up the department before his retirement in 1984.

The Advertisement Manager in 1984 was Mr Stuart Burkinshaw, assisted by Mr Stephen Hare and Mr Michael Hutton.

★ ★ ★ ★

In times of industrial unrest, it was inevitably the advertising services which were the most sorely missed. For example, it was difficult to arrange a funeral efficiently without announcing the details through the columns, while the inability to place vital public notices held up many plans. During most strikes, however, it was found possible to keep the continuity going through some sort of emergency publication. It was a near thing during the printers' strike of 1921, when for a day or two the news had to be typewritten in Dock Street, photographed on zinc plates and printed on the rotary machines in Whitefriargate; and in the General Strike of 1926 similar difficulties were faced and overcome.

Strike-hit again in 1959, the *Hull Daily Mail* issued a duplicated sheet packed on both sides with local news, which was eagerly snapped up by queues of people at street sellers' stands and newsagents' shops. At a later stage in the dispute, makeshift arrangements enabled the *Hull Daily Mail* to be printed again, this time in a reduced size, but containing local and national news and pictures. This effort resulted in a Socialist member of Hull City Council moving the exclusion of the Press from a meeting of the Health Committee. He did not find a seconder. By the time the stoppage ended, the printed edition had increased from four to eight pages and included display advertisements.

Industrial disputes have since stopped the presses from time to time, but never for very long. Usually it proved possible to bring out a modified edition of the paper – often a very creditable one – masterminded by the Editor and as few as three senior journalists.

At one time, Christmas Day and Good Friday were the only non--publication days, apart from Sundays, but today a sprinkling of Bank Holidays is observed throughout the year. Records show that the staff had a day off on Peace Day, 1919, and on one of the Victory Days in 1945.

The Press Ball was a major annual event in Hull's social calendar with its eagerly sought prizes.

The entrance hall of the Jameson Street premises.

Sport – A Growth Industry

'As part of a nation who love sport so much that they produce the most vehement arguments about it, there is little surprise that the people of Hull and the surrounding areas should demand satisfaction, as it were, from their newspaper,' writes Brian Taylor. It was recognised 100 years ago with the promise of 'special sporting news' in a handbill which heralded the arrival of the *Hull Daily Mail* in 1885. The promise was kept with a wide and detailed coverage in national and local sporting arenas. But it has been a promise which has proved extremely difficult to live up to as the years have gone by.

As any sporting student will know, the scene has changed out of all recognition in 100 years, and the major factor is not the professionalism which was then beginning to stick out a hesitant, palm-uppermost hand, but the sheer extent of sport. Leisure is now a multi-million pound business, for the simple reasons that people have the money and the time to enjoy it as spectators and participants.

Indeed, it would not be difficult to make out a case that the nation's decline in performance can be blamed on the diversification of interest which has sprung up in the years since sportsmen ruled as convincingly as Britannia.

'Sporting Intelligence', as it was curiously entitled in bygone days, sprang from a close affinity to gambling, and, of course, that intimate link has by no means diminished, although the sport of kings, like just about all else, needs huge injections of outside help and internal taxation to keep its hooves off the slope to ruination. All the other traditional sports of a century ago now need that aid, collectively and individually, but what has been spawned in the meantime by an increasingly leisure-conscious population is a multitude of pastimes which once barely rated mention, and now attract thousands.

★ ★ ★ ★

Indeed, such is the range of things unknown to the sports fan of a century ago that it is hard to know where to start and end in trying to draw the contrast between then and now. Canoeing, hang-gliding, boating in its many forms, basketball, gymnastics and jogging, to mention just half a dozen, are now available – and enjoyed – by thousands. A hundred years ago, you might as well have said 'computer' or 'video'! It is difficult to sustain them all, and no less hard for newspapers to gratify the keenness of their followers by giving them coverage. Despite the advances that have been made in newspaper production, it is too often the case that the cherry is not big enough for all who want a bite of it.

That particular pressure has compacted ever more tightly as the years have rolled by, to add to the day-to-day needs of recording the events of a district which has always been heavily inclined to sport, and has had its share of thrills and thrillers.

Over most of those years, of course, the greatest demand on the *Hull Daily Mail's* sports columns has been made by Hull City, the soccer club, and Hull FC and Kingston Rovers, the two Rugby League sides. It is arguable that the intense rivalry between the Airlie Birds and the Robins has fired the city's sporting interest to a pitch reached by no one else. Both have reaped a rich harvest of honours from the game and supplied a succession of talented and characterful exponents whose names ripple from supporters' lips with the same frequency that they reached the headlines.

But such are the troughs and peaks of sporting life that it has been necessary to chronicle, too, the times when both came perilously close to extinction.

Happily, they survived. Not only that, they grew to such stature that in the past few years their dominance led to Hull being dubbed 'Rugby League City'.

And it is from that, perhaps, that the greatest irony in a century of sports reporting came. In 1980, the long-cherished dream of a Rugby League Cup Final between these two at Wembley was realised. But on this day of all days, there was no *Hull Daily Mail* to report it. Industrial action kept the paper off the streets . . . and a posse of journalists and photographers geared up to fever pitch over the preceding weeks suffered the biggest frustration of their lives.

Tigers' Finest Hour

Thankfully, that has not been a too-frequent occurrence, and, Saturday after Saturday, there has been the specialist *Sports Mail* to back up the day-to-day coverage.

That paper, started in 1913, reached its peak in the early years after the 1939-45 War. The re-emergence of sport was a welcome relief from the days of anxiety, terror and austerity . . . for in those days the favours which fans wore proudly camouflaged the Ration Book in their pocket. It was said that production in the re-emerging postwar industries could be measured by the success of the local sides. It was, at that time, a morale-booster of immense proportions. Industry in Hull must have drawn huge benefit, if that was the case. Shortly before Hitler plunged Europe into a contest that no-one was keen to join, Hull City had made plans to move from their out-moded Anlaby Road ground to a new stadium at Boothferry Park. Prophetically, in view of the subsequent advances in those particular fields, the site had been a golf course and a cricket ground. The move to Boothferry Park was virtually forced on the new-look Hull City.

Around the time that Hitler was planning to take Germany to the top of the World League table, the Tigers had been one of the sides whose concentration on defence led to a major change in the offside law. But between 1939 and 1945 there was no defence – only great fortitude against the Luftwaffe attacks which levelled the city – and its soccer ground.

Fashioned at a time when building was restricted, Boothferry Park was perforce somewhat primitive in the mid-1940's. But, to echo Churchill, Britain's erstwhile captain, the decade which followed the war was the Tigers' finest hour. It was difficult at that time for the reporters of the day to keep track of the records which the team and their supporters created. In those days, Saturday afternoon was THE sports time for Hull's Big Three, as they came to be known. Hull's eagerness to follow them and read about them led to the *Sports Mail's* circulation soaring to the 70,000 mark.

For a variety of reasons, that peak may never be reached again, but it is a tribute to the sporting interest of Hull fans that the specialist sporting paper had remained a viable proposition at a time when, all over the North, contemporary Greens, Pinks, Buffs and Blues have paled into oblivion. *The Sports Mail Green* is one at the few survivors of its kind.

★　★　★　★

That, then, is the centre-stage of a century of sports reporting by the *Hull Daily Mail*.

It would be impossible to draw up a cast list that was anything like comprehensive. For every Batten, Harrison and Whiteley, for every Osborne, West and Millward and for every Mills, Hill and Wagstaff, any fan – and any headline writer – can conjure up a dozen or more names of like stature. Indeed, the more one toys with that idea, the more one realises just how deep is that 100-year store of talent which has graced the playing-fields of Hull's senior clubs.

Their deeds were recorded by a collection of characters who were just as diverse, and in styles which have changed as drastically as the tactics of their respective games.

Reporting used to be most impersonal and matter-of-fact. Steadily, there evolved a demand for a lighter approach, more gossip and background. Then, as the specialist reporter was born, came critical assessment. Ultimately, in the razzmatazz, ballyhoo and sponsorship into which sport was driven as a means of survival, the stage was reached where it was no longer just a question of who scored, but what his wife wore at the celebration dinner afterwards. It is always debatable whether newspapers lead or follow these peculiar winds of change in our society. Suffice it to say that they, too, are faced with the need to survive.

★　★　★　★

While the Big Three took their ordained place in the centre-stage, the back-drop to the sporting scene was not without its share of the limelight from time to time.

In a community whose lifestyle was rough and ready, because that was the nature of the industries from which they eked a hard but often happy existence, it is not surprising that boxing was dear to their hearts. The City and surrounding areas produced countless boxers of class and many another fighter who could win plaudits for his guts, a characteristic greatly admired by those for whom it was a workaday virtue as they brought home the fish which was part of the country's staple diet. Hull was always a great centre for professional boxing, and, even now, it flourishes briefly from time to time. Mainly, though, the city's interest is reflected in a welter of amateur clubs, who have produced some outstanding exponents in their own sphere.

Cricket has always been a difficult game to maintain. A welter of equipment, a specially-prepared ground, vagaries of the weather, and, socially, an indeterminate time factor, are some of the drawbacks. Sadly, Hull's senior side have fallen from the heights which once made them the most feared side in the Yorkshire League, yet, down the scale, there has been a burgeoning of other competitive organizations . . . federations, alliances, call them what you will.

It is only 50 years since cricket was first played in Hull on a Sunday. It created a big enough furore to be worthy of front-page space in the *Hull Daily Mail* of that time. Now, Sunday cricket – and a host of other sports – is an integral part of the leisure scene.

Golf was once thought of as a game for the rich, yet more than 50 years ago Hull Corporation established their first municipal course, and this was soon followed by another. Both have flourished and new private courses have been laid out to add to those already established. The game has become one of the top participant sports in the land.

Hull has always been fond of tennis, too, probably because, in the days before the University bulged outwards, the YPI club at Ferens Recreation Ground boasted more courts that the All England Club at Wimbledon! That facility attracted many senior tournaments to the city and there was abundant talent for league tournaments and the Yorkshire teams. Like so many sports, tennis is far removed from those days, with ambitious coaching schemes into which youngsters are tempted almost as soon as they are big enough to hold a racket.

* * * *

In a city of such flat topography, it is not at all surprising that cycling should be popular. Most people were led into it as a natural development, for in less affluent times the bike was the accepted way of getting about.

In modern times, Billy Holmes was the name most frequently tapped out on the sports journalists' typewriters, but before the turn of the century, when they wrote longhand in heavy black pencil, it was Jack Stocks who captured the cycling headlines. What was the feat of this Post Office clerk? He rode his bike 25 miles within the hour. Hull will never rival the Continent where cycling is virtually a religion, but it has made its mark by staging extremely prestigious events.

A mere three years after the *Hull Daily Mail* was launched, there was the opening of Hedon Racecourse to report. Now, though, the area's centre for the sport of kings is the long-established course on Beverley's Westwood, where old traditions abound and that so-necessary local support helps to preserve them.

Runners on two legs have had their feats plentifully recorded over the years as well, some of them reaching the Olympian peaks scaled most recently by Sue Hearnshaw.

Those are the heady days for even the most cynical of sports journalists, all of whom, from their memories – and their files – could spread before you sufficient names to keep you talking for the next 100 years.

A cross-section of men who, in their own sphere, were as talented and characterful as the people they wrote about, have put into print millions upon millions of words over this first century. The men who sent their despatches on 'flimsies' attached to a pigeon's leg have long since gone. Their successors have seen technological advances parallel to the improvement and extension in all branches of sport.

But, way back in 1885, when that handbill heralding the new *Hull Daily Mail* promised 'Special Sporting News', no-one could forecast how important it would be to keep that promise. No-one knew how important sport and leisure time was to become. From those early days, there has developed a breed of specialists who have emerged from *noms de plume* of classical or local notation to signed articles and an accompanying photograph.

For them it is now even more difficult to forecast what lies ahead in the next 100 years. For the moment, 'Special Sporting News' is still their aim. And, to a man, they will hope that in 2085 someone will write that they and their successors kept the promise – even if the Martians have just won the Ashes, Venus have got to the Jules Rimet Trophy, and that upstart from Jupiter has set an Inter-Galactic Games record of 6.5 seconds in the 100 metres!

Author Barbara Robinson, who wrote the Jane Humber column, with Brian Taylor, later John Humber.

From 'House and Home' to Women's Lib

From the first, the *Hull Daily Mail* contained items which were clearly designed to appeal specially to its women readers – 'Social Scraps', giving snippets of news about Queen Victoria's health and about the doings of society personalities, details of local social and charitable events and the like. In the early 1890's, however, the Editor's wife Mrs E. S. Lewis, began writing a weekly feature under the title, 'House and Home'. Described as 'our lady contributor', she signed herself 'Mother Humber', a name that was to mean much to the poor and elderly in the ensuing years.

'House and Home' was, however, primarily a shopping column, giving full details of where the best consumer goods and materials of the day could be found – and obviously intended as an advertisement-puller as well as a service to women readers. The solid mass of fashion notes with which it began each Thursday would probably, even then, have brought a frown to the brow of any member of that growing army of *femmes savantes* who were beginning to infiltrate the colleges and the professions, and had long since started clamouring for the vote and other rights. But today those meticulously detailed descriptions of the garments of the period provide an invaluable source of information for the costume historian; and one assumes that, though similar features today may bore the bikini-panties off the T-shirt-and-jeans brigade and infuriate their more militant sisters, they will have similar value for the museum curators of the future.

At all events, it was not long before Mother Humber was inserting into her columns telling little comments about the manners and customs of the day, blended in among the cooking and household hints and advice on how to manage the servants.

She commented on women smoking, on complaints about inefficiency among the recently-appointed women Post Office clerks, saying that they must not take advantage of the fact that they were women! She told the story of an American writer who took a job as a domestic servant and then wrote about her experiences. Even Mother Humber's shopping excursions were not without their little touches of poetic philosophy: 'A woman setting out shopping is like a voyager on a far-off cruise,' she wrote. 'She is setting sail into unknown regions where a thousand possibilities await her.'

Some advice she gave in 1894 still holds good today: 'How often parents either consciously or unconsciously, influence their children towards a right or wrong marriage. If, for instance, children are spoken of as a "necessary evil", that household cares are only a burden, that life would have been better if they had not married, this root of selfishness will soon spread its poison, not only into the present home but probably into the homes of the next generation.'

Her attitude to the status of women appeared to be that they should seize every existing opportunity for fulfilment, using and developing the powers they already possessed, before pressing for more. 'The revolution that has spread through the feminine world has not necessarily detracted from its womanliness,' wrote Mother Humber. 'Quite the contrary, it has raised women to be true women – beings with hearts and brains instead of prettily-dressed, empty-headed dolls.' And again, 'I wonder why women take so small a place in the production of dramas, operas, burlesques, comedy and farce? Surely, if women can become BAs, Senior Wranglers, doctors and novelists, they should much more frequently be able to write something of interest for the stage.'

Great stuff! For these were the days of Ibsen and Shaw, whose ideas had obviously penetrated into the British provinces. 'House and Home' was well written. Mother Humber was a well-educated, well-informed woman with a strong social conscience. She read the national newspapers as well as the journal edited by her husband, and commented on what she found there.

★ ★ ★ ★

She gave her opinion that child-batterers should have a taste of their own medicine. She slammed into Sir Mark Sykes when he suggested that old age pensions were unnecessary, and that the nation should rather look after its young. And in 1907-8, appalled by the poverty and misery she saw around her as the plushy, prosperous Edwardian era was drawing to a close, she gathered a group of like-minded friends around her and, with the help of the *Hull Daily Mail*, which provided office accommodation, staff and publicity, she started the Mother Humber Fund.

Throughout the next 60 years, the fund, re-titled the Mother Humber Memorial Fund after her death, was to bring relief to thousands of needy people throughout the city, operating first from the *Hull Daily Mail* offices and later from premises in Spring Bank. Shortly after World War II, the fund ran a small residential home near Pearson Park, on Beverley Road, for elderly women who had been bombed out of their homes, and this was eventually handed over to the local authority. As the Welfare State gradually took over the job of providing for the needs of the population, the fund concentrated more on the elderly, who had been somewhat left behind in the postwar benefit bonanza – and many of them, in any case, did not know how to claim their rights, or were too proud to do so.

As has already been mentioned, 'House and Home' was suspended during the early part of the First World War, and when it reappeared it was signed 'Portia'. This was the pen-name of Mrs Charles Watson – another *Mail* wife, whose husband was Deputy Editor. Like her predecessor, Portia was a strong--minded, well-informed woman, and she was also a member of the Board of Guardians. She, too, knew how the other half lived, and, although she handled her fair share of fashion and household notes, she did not scruple to tackle such matters as the proposed banning of German literature and music after the war and the denial of aid to starving German children. The arts, she said, were 'all part of the culture and civilisation that we were trying to defend'. And all needy children must be fed and cared for. Portia also demanded to know why there were no women speakers in Hull Literary and Philosophical Society's 1920 list. She suggested clothes repair shops for the increasing number of working women who did not have time to do fiddling repairs at home; and she tackled the sordid problem of women and their children hanging about the Hull docks area.

★　★　★　★

Portia's reign overlapped those of many other women feature writers in the expanding newspapers of the 1920's and 30's. After 1918, the first women staff journalists, as opposed to freelance contributors, began to be taken on the pay-roll, and, in addition to carrying out general reporting duties, they were also assigned to the collection of material for special women's features, assembled and laid out by a sub-editor under the by-lines of 'Babette' and, later, 'Miss Humber'.

Among the women columnists of that era was Mrs Dixon, remembered for her 'earphones' hairstyle, popular at the time, the hair being braided and then coiled over the ears. Then there were Joan Blackburn, a member of the family of aviation pioneers whose works were based at Brough, Hilda Marchant and Audrey Whiting, both of whom went on to make international reputations for themselves in journalism, Stella Schofield, Doris Allen, and, best known of all, perhaps, Peggy Shapero, who became extremely popular in the district as a personality as well as a column-writer.

In the 1920's and 30's, the feature pages of the paper were crammed with items of all kinds, including a beauty article signed by film star Madeleine Carroll, and numerous other syndicated features on dressmaking, cookery and hobbies. Peggy Shapero married fellow-journalist and playwright Michael Walsh in 1943, and they went to live in Manchester. After a short but extremely active and joyful married life, during which they wrote and broadcast together and entertained lavishly, their happiness was marred when Peggy had a stroke from which she never fully recovered. She spent her last years in hospital, where Michael visited her every day. It was one of journalism's sweetest and saddest romances.

★　★　★　★

During the rest of the war, with its shortages of staff and materials, women's columns were put together more or less regularly, but were not associated with any one personality. As the war ended – when, paradoxically, newsprint became even more scarce – they disappeared altogether, and paragraphs about women personalities were included in 'John Humber's' notes, which were kept going.

Among the women who wrote for the paper regularly during the 1930's and 40's, mention should perhaps be made of Clara Simpson, whose Patience Strong-type 'Thoughts for the Day' were either loved or hated by readers according to their degree of sophistication and literary taste!

It was news reporter Marjorie Stephenson who re-started the 'Miss Humber' column in 1949, side by side with John Humber's on what was then the 'Leader Page'. Mrs Stephenson later returned to her home town of Grimsby, where she joined the *Evening Telegraph*. Meanwhile, Miss Roma Sanders was appointed, and she held the post until November, 1968, though her later years were marred by illness. Roma Sanders was a first-class journalist with a thorough knowledge of the origins and structure of women's organisations. A Welsh woman with a keen sense of humour, she was a popular speaker in the area. She worked closely with the Mother Humber Fund, drawing attention in her column to the plight in which many elderly people still found themselves in the 1950's, and she personally collected and distributed many cash donations and parcels of food and clothing for them.

She was also the *Hull Daily Mail's* first true Woman Editor, sub-editing and proof-reading her own copy, selecting, sizing and captioning pictures and supervising the make-up of the column in the Composing Room. She died in 1968 at the early age of 57, and was succeeded by Barbara Duncanson, (later Robinson) who, along with Iris Segal, had deputised for long periods during Miss Sanders's illness.

By 1974, the title 'Miss Humber' had acquired a somewhat quaint and old-fashioned ring, so the lady was given a forename – Jane. Though the feature today may seem very different in outward appearance from the 'House and Home' of the 1890's, the two had much in common. The aim was still to give a woman's very special viewpoint on the world, and to blend serious comment and human-interest stories with a little bit of harmless fun and a spot of useful domestic information in the form of fashion pictures and household hints, though the balance is, of course, very different now.

We like to think that as many men as women read 'A Woman's View' – but then, we suspect that their great-grandfathers also perused 'House and Home'!

★　★　★　★

Over the years, there have also been a number of male columnists, including 'Observer', who kept his readers informed of happenings on the East – or 'Christian side' – of North Bridge, so called because of the number of churches in the area. In the early years of the century, 'Humberside Echoes' was signed 'White Friar', and another weekly column, on town topics, was contributed by 'Juniper Junior'.

By the time the Humberside Echoes theme was re-started in the early 1930's, the newspaper had moved to Jameson Street, so 'White Friar' was no longer appropriate, and 'John Humber' was born. There have, to date, been seven 'regenerations' of that popular character. The first, in 1931, was John Birch, one of the staff 'taken over' with the opposition *Evening News*. The second was Tom Geraghty, doubling the role of Assistant Editor. Then came Arthur Brewer, who was succeeded in turn by Ian Stockdale, Michael Thompson, and Roy Woodcock. At the time of writing, John Humber was Brian Taylor, former Sports Editor of the *Mail*.

Postwar Changes

Peace brought changes in managerial and editorial leadership. In 1947, Thomas Blakie Mackim took over the editorial chair from W. S. Robinson, who retired but continued to take a keen interest in the newspaper up to the time of his death.

Mr Mackim, a Scot by birth, came to Hull from Leicester. A firm editor, he was a superb typographer and layout man, and under his guidance the appearance of the paper was further modernised. Shortly after his arrival, Mr John T. Paterson came from Lincoln to succeed Mr H. V. Weller as General Manager. And Mr George Smith, who bridged the gap, is also remembered with affection. Mr Weller left for Edinburgh, but died soon afterwards at a tragically early age. Mr Mackim retired in 1960, and was followed as Managing Editor by Mr J. H. Giles, of Grimsby. In 1966, Mr Giles vacated the editorial chair in favour of Mr James Humble, moving on to a group consultancy post in Exeter, and Mr Humble held the editorship until 1973, when he replaced Mr Paterson on his retirement as General Manager.

The next Editor was Mr J. A. Whitfield, who spent his long journalistic career entirely in the service of newspapers on the North and South Banks of the Humber. Mr Whitfield's early experience was gained in North Lincolnshire, and he then completed a number of years as News Editor of the *Hull Daily Mail* before taking up the editorship of the *Grimsby Evening Telegraph*, returning to the *Hull Daily Mail* as Editor in, 1973.

On Jack Whitfield's a retirement in 1976, Staffordshire-born Bill Sneyd was appointed Editor, and on the retirement of Mr Humble, who also took up a Group consultancy, Mr T. A. Griffin took over as General Manager, to be succeeded in January, 1981, by Mr Jim Craig, who moved over the Humber from Grimsby. Mr Sneyd left the *Hull Daily Mail* in September, 1984, to study computer technology with a view to taking up another post within Northcliffe Newspapers Group. He was succeeded by Mr Michael G. Wood, former Editor of the *Derby Evening Telegraph*. Mr Wood began his career as a sports reporter, and was appointed Sports Editor of the *Leicester Mercury* and Editor of the weekly *Sports Mercury* in 1966.

After spells with the *Hereford Evening News* and *Kent Messenger* Group and work as a freelance, writing and broadcasting for Leicester News Service, Mr Wood returned to the *Mercury* as Production Editor for its free newspaper. He became Assistant News Editor of the *Mercury*, worked briefly as Assistant Chief Sub-Editor, and was then appointed Deputy News Editor. In 1979, Mr Wood moved to Grimsby as Assistant Editor and his appointment to the Derby newspaper was made in 1981.

Other members of the editorial team who are following us into our second century include Assistant Editor Keith Perry, News Editor Keith Seacroft, his deputy, Kenneth Farrier, Assistant News Editor Paul W. Williamson, and County News

Editor Ian D. Stockdale. Chief Sub-Editor is Dennis Sissons, his deputy Roy Woodcock; the *Lincolnshire and South Humberside Times* is edited by Derek Hilton. Mr Brian Perrington is responsible for the management of the *Star*, which is edited by Deborah Lockwood. Other key figures are Feature Editors Stuart Russell and David Carsberg.

★   ★   ★   ★

One more boardroom transaction remains to be recorded: In October, 1963, to release cash in preparation for a big expansion programme, Provincial Newspapers, who now own, among many other journals, the *Yorkshire Post and Evening Post*, a number of smaller Yorkshire and Humberside publications and a group of national periodicals including the famous *Punch*, sold their remaining shares in Hull and Grimsby Newspapers to Associated Newspapers, the parent company of the Northcliffe Group. 'Harley Drayton had a talk with Lord Rothermere, and the deal went through expeditiously and cordially,' records Guy Schofield. 'Rothermere bought United's 49 per cent for £1,700,000 in cash – a handsome lump sum for the kitty.' The Hull newspapers, in common with other group publications throughout the country, are now administered under the Associated Newspapers umbrella by Northcliffe.

IT SEEMS A LITTLE SAD, PERHAPS, THAT THIS RECORD OF A CENTURY'S DEVELOPMENT OF A CITY AND ITS NEWSPAPER SHOULD HAVE TO END AT A TIME WHEN HULL, HUMBERSIDE, AND THE COUNTRY AS A WHOLE, ARE GOING THROUGH A RECESSION, WITH HEADLINES RECORDING MASSIVE UNEMPLOYMENT.

BUT WHERE THERE'S LIFE, THEY SAY, THERE'S HOPE; AND THE *HULL DAILY MAIL* IS OPTIMISTIC THAT THE FUTURE HOLDS GREAT THINGS FOR THIS REGION.

WHEN THE SLEEPING GIANT BEGINS TO STIR, WE ARE CONFIDENT THAT WE SHALL BE HERE TO RECORD THE AWAKENING.

A New Home

By the 1960's, rumour was rife around the city that the *Hull Daily Mail* was seeking a site for a new office, and there was much public speculation as to where the chosen location would be.

A central position was vital, to link up with communication services. Moreover, the public had acquired a sentimental attachment to the Jameson Street building. 'Meet you in the Hull Daily Mail front entrance,' was a popular assignation. Young couples came shyly to place their engagement and wedding announcements and later, triumphantly, to record the births of their children, their offsprings' examination successes, and various anniversaries and other family landmarks. The bereaved found comfort from sympathetic staff when they had difficulty over a death notice or memorial tribute.

Various sites were considered, and finally, in the Autumn of 1977, Hull and Grimsby Newspapers acquired the site familiarly known as 'Blundell's Corner', at the junction of Beverley Road and Spring Bank, with a view to future development

The site was later leased to National Car Parks, and up to the time of writing of this history, the date of development is uncertain.

Blundell's Corner at the junction of Spring Bank (left) and Beverley Road (right), showing the vacant space where the new Mail *offices were to be built. A famous hostelry, The Zoological, now demolished, was still standing when this photograph was taken.*

The new Mail building at Blundell's Corner in a style quite new to Hull.

The Story to Date – Blundell's Corner

By John Markham

(This chapter is largely based on information given by Roy Woodcock, Editor of *The Journal* and Regional Magazines and Supplements Editor, and Angus Young, Local Government Reporter of the *Mail*. I am greatly indebted to them).

Moving from Jameson Street to Blundell's Corner, Beverley Road, in October 1989 meant more than a new location. It was a cultural shock. A Special Souvenir Supplement published on the occasion described this newest chapter in the story of the newspaper's progress: 'From a press which clattered its way through 4,000 copies an hour to the very latest in printing technology which, when it gets cracking, can whistle out 700 a minute.'

The Jameson Street building, occupied since 1926, miraculously survived the Blitz, but had become increasingly inadequate, a rabbit warren of rooms, a complex period piece of nooks and crannies, corridors, stairs and clanking metal lifts. It was the archetypal newspaper office of old black and white films, the air so dense with cigarette smoke that walls were nicotine-yellow and dustbin fires were frequent.

Reporters used the Star of the West in West Street as their drinking hole while the Editor patronised the bar of the White Horse Hotel. To supplement accommodation a building further along Jameson Street had been brought into use but, as car ownership became more common, there was no way of increasing parking space in the crowded city-centre site.

The demands of new technology made the move essential – and urgent. Computers were revolutionising printing. The old press, which had faithfully produced newspapers recording events both national and local for so many years, even during the ravages of war, had no place in the world of the new media. It had become essential to have a facility for full-colour printing, a need which the Jameson Street press could not fulfil. The plans of staff eager to introduce new ideas were constantly frustrated.

But, even if logic made a move necessary, there were still regrets at leaving such an atmospheric place. In spite of its deficiencies, there was great affection for a building, with many happy memories, a strong sense of camaraderie, even of being part of a family. There were high demarcation lines between journalists and printers but this division disappeared in a crisis when they pulled together as a team.

For local people it meant the loss of a landmark. The *Mail* clock was as unmistakable a meeting place in Hull as the Victoria Station clock was in London and the attractive recessed entrance with its displays of photographs a pleasant spot to wait, at least for a while. Inside were more pictures and files of recent copies of the paper in a marble-floored foyer. Delft tiles on the walls included a decorative panel of sailing ships. Roy Woodcock has sentimentally retained one which he uses as a paperweight.

The old building had a major asset. It was located in the very heart of the city in a street crowded with pedestrians, cars and buses passing all day long, the right environment for a newspaper which played a crucial role in the life of the community. Blundell's Corner was only a walk away, but it was just off centre, beyond a busy junction. Yet the decision to move there has proved to be right. If it had been delayed longer the likely outcome would have been no option but to accept a site further out of the town.

Inevitably there was a feeling that continuity had been lost but detailed planning helped to ease the transition from old to new. Before Blundell's Corner was occupied a team of planners had been at work. Almost all the existing staff moved, including some compositors, and with a certain apprehension but success the new press had produced a dummy run of the paper.

Instead of the, sometimes awkward, intimacy of Jameson Street, there was now the spaciousness of an open-plan office and completely new working conditions, to which staff adjusted with surprising speed. Smoking while you work had gone for ever. A special area was designated for smoking and to conform to new legislation even that had later to be abandoned.

Change had been in the air long before the move, but plans in the pipeline were now easier to implement. The new location stimulated further changes in the style of the paper both visually and in contents. One difference which had made an immediate impact was adopting the tabloid format in 1986. Throughout the 1980s and 90s there was constant innovation, a readiness to try new approaches and a series of re-designs. After experimenting with a modern masthead it was eventually decided to revert to a traditional typeface. Sometimes change goes full circle.

Though always referred to as the *Hull Daily Mail*, its correct title was *Daily Mail*. Now it became officially *Hull Daily Mail*, though with further developments this in turn changed to the *Mail*. The increasing number of people who lived in the East Riding led in 2002 to the launch of the *East Riding Mail*, especially geared towards them, as a sister paper to the *Hull Mail*.

The fundamental aim underlying all these changes was to create a more lively style, a paper which was better to look at and more appealing to readers accustomed to the eye-catching techniques of modern advertisements. Its character also underwent an evolution. For a long time it had conveyed the image of a conservative, conventional publication produced by a pair of safe hands. It developed into a more pro-active campaigning paper, seeing itself as a key player in the local community involved in local issues, prepared, when circumstances required, to be controversial. Readers' letters were given prominence and reader participation was given a new dimension with the 1998 launch of the website, which invited immediate feedback through comment on the paper's contents: John Meehan, Editor since 1998, has played a vigorous role in the re-branding of the *Mail;* he is an enthusiast for innovation with a dynamic hands-on approach to all these new situations and possibilities.

Social changes in the region served by the *Mail* were just as great as those in Blundell's Corner itself and the paper had to adapt to its readers' lifestyle. Many were more affluent than previous generations of their families, their leisure time was spent in a wider variety of pursuits and far more ate out, becoming familiar with foods which their parents and grandparents had never tasted – often never heard of. The *Mail* had to respond to these new circumstances and new demands; it now had the technical ability to do so. One outcome was *The Journal*, a large format, full-colour glossy magazine, first published in 1989, supplied free to homes in selected areas (but also on sale), with editorial contents and advertisements aimed at those interested in homes, gardens, interior design, restaurants, cars and entertainment. Editor Roy Woodcock admits his luck in having the best job in the world, trying out expensive cars and eating good meals, all for the ultimate edification of his readers. A very popular feature, Downey's Diary (started by former staff member Paul Downey), consists of several pages of photographs of local social and charitable events. To have your picture in *The Journal* has become a status symbol.

The *Mail* itself reflected the interests which now featured more prominently in readers' lives and The Guide to restaurants, films, other forms of entertainment and cultural events, a Saturday supplement, went on to win a national industry award.

Regional newspapers have had to reconsider their role, their very *raison d'être*. No longer do people wait for the newspaper to bring them up to date with the latest happenings. As well as a 24-hour televised news service, there are regular news broadcasts on local radio and television, competitors to the *Mail* not just for news stories but also in some cases for advertising. Technology, in particular the Internet, has altered the way information is transmitted and received. This is all a world away from the parochial local newspapers which concentrated on making an accurate record of the names of mourners at funerals and helpers at church bazaars.

The editorial contents of the *Mail* now had to be presented in a livelier style, to be 'easier on the eye' and easier to navigate, acquiring more of the character of a magazine. This was in no way a policy of dumbing-down but a reflection of the shift in evaluating news with which regional newspapers have to cope. A judgement has to be made on which news is more suited to video and which to the printed page. Newspapers have had to re-establish their identity and their purpose. The staid image had to go. In its place came a livelier approach to local issues, a willingness to campaign (the need for government financial help for Hull following the disastrous floods of 2007 was one example), the courage to be controversial and a determination to be seen as an influential partner in the community.

The letter page was re-designed to encourage discussion on topical issues and the pioneering website launched in 1998 offered an opportunity for two-way communication, with readers able to respond immediately with their comments on items in that day's issue.

In 2006 video journalism, with news reviews, was introduced to the website, making the *Mail* the first regional newspaper in the country to offer this service. The same year an innovative property website was added to the services available. Though the familiar green *Sports Mail*, rushed out on Saturday afternoons, has fallen a victim to the new media world, sports news is still as eagerly devoured as it ever was. A pull-out Sports section is published with each Monday's *Mail* and a Sports website, Sportshull, was introduced in 2007. Other supplements issued with the *Mail* are Female (Tuesday), Jobs and The Business (Wednesday), Homes-Property Guide (Thursday), Motors (Friday) and The Guide (Saturday). Each year has brought something new. In 2008 the *Mail* launched its unique user-generated website, Your Mail, where residents of East Yorkshire and beyond can discuss local events, debate current issues or post photographs or news. Users can share news in Your Patch, manage their own groups in All Yours or create Your Family pages. In the first year lengthy debates were conducted on topics ranging from national events to Yorkshire food.

Even if the *Sports Mail* has gone, the *Mail* has continued with other offshoots, the 'freebies' with contents aimed at specific areas. Their titles and format have evolved over the years. The *Hull Star* and the *Beverley Star* were succeeded by the five-edition *Target* and, after the acquisition of the *Beverley Advertiser*, the two Beverley papers were merged. Subsequently the full *Advertiser* series was launched. Read by 275,000 adults, it has more readers than any other newspaper within the total *Mail* marketing area. In a rapidly changing world the lure of nostalgia is potent. The *Flashback* series reproducing photographs and stories from the *Mail's* archives has a continuing popularity, while local history and nostalgia are the themes of daily columns in the *Mail* itself, The Living Past and Flashback Daily.

The re-focusing of the *Mail*, the new technology and changes in its appearance and philosophy have had their impact on staff. The old-style journalist, still the stereotype of some television programmes, who spends his entire career at one ramshackle office, a jack-of-all-trades who relies on tip-offs from carefully cultivated contacts, is now an endangered, if not entirely extinct, species. Staff turnover has been higher (though less so in the past ten years) and fewer entrants are school-leavers. The majority are university graduates who have opted for a journalistic career and completed a post-graduate professional course. There is, though, some revival of a former tradition with an expressed interest in recruiting more local people to the editorial staff. *Mail* journalists are often assigned specialist roles in certain areas, for example, in local government, health, education, crime and the courts, while reporters based at Beverley also cover a wide range of subjects across the region.

Not everything has gone to plan. The new printing press, which had been such a strong factor in the decision to move to Blundell's Corner, proved unreliable. A number of breakdowns, one of the worst situations a newspaper can experience, led to the even more radical decision to close the Hull works and have printing done in Grimsby. More recently, printing has moved from Grimsby to the Midlands.

Accompanying these developments has been another major change, one which has not always been easy for long-time readers to accept. The *Mail* is no longer an evening paper. Editions for both Hull and the East Riding are published in the morning and this in turn necessitates an overnight deadline. All this is an indication of the media revolution's consequences for regional newspapers in a world where local news is more often initially received through radio and television, leaving the press to follow up relevant stories with background information and further comment.

It is no exaggeration to use the word 'revolution'. Once everything was geared round print. Now everything is done electronically with instant transmission of made-up pages by the pressing of a button, a complete contrast to Angus Young's experience in his first job as a young reporter on the *Beverley Guardian* in the 1980s. Typewriters making carbon copies were the most up-to-date technology in use. All the stories for the next edition were placed in an envelope which Angus took to Beverley Bus Station and handed to Horace, the Inspector, so that they could be safely despatched on the next bus for printing in Driffield.

Change is often a matter of evolution, not linked to any specific date, yet there have been some years with a particular significance in the *Mail* chronology. In 1998, as already noted, the website was launched: far more than a newspaper on the web – an interactive information service. The following year the Duke of Edinburgh, in Hull in connection with the 700th anniversary of the granting of a charter by Edward I, honoured Blundell's Corner with a visit. He is a man who does not confine himself to the expected royal platitudes. 'What do you do about literals [misprints]?' he asked. 'We don't have any,' he was told.

In 2003 a £1.7 million programme to refurbish the Blundell's Corner headquarters began and in 2004 the *Mail* underwent a huge branding exercise so that it could send out 'a consistent and coherent message' about its range of diverse products. By the end of 2003 the monthly electronic audience reached 97,000 and by 2007 the monthly figure was 158,860.

These developments were all powered by the realisation that a newspaper – particularly a regional one – cannot be a remote publication which descends from on high. The *Mail* is a two-way medium of communication in a culture where readers regard it as normal to participate and make their own contribution.

It operates in a difficult world with competition from other forms of media and from another regional daily, the *Yorkshire Post*. Confidence in the future is, however, boosted by tangible proof that the *Mail* is proceeding on the right lines. In 2003 it was named as Northcliffe Newspaper Group's Publishing Centre of the Year and in 2003, 2004 and 2006 it won the Yorkshire Daily Newspaper of the Year award. One advertisement in the *Mail* reaches 140,000 local people, 37% of the local population.

These are challenging times for all newspapers. The Internet will continue to change the environment in which they operate. The staff of the *Mail* know they must embrace change, be relevant to the community and offer something which the rest of the media cannot provide.

A newspaper has many advantages. It is still a very convenient way of receiving information, requiring neither expensive equipment nor technical skill. It is something you can hold in your hand, read at your own speed and refer to whenever you wish. As the computer buffs would say, it is user-friendly. Settling down in a comfortable chair with your local newspaper remains one of life's simple, unspoilt pleasures.

The Mail, *which employs over 400 people, mostly at Blundell's Corner, Hull, and in Beverley, is part of Northcliffe Media's North-East region, which also includes Grimsby, Scunthorpe and Lincoln centre. The Hull Managing Director is also the North-East Regional Managing Director.*

Index